Healing from School

Reclaim Your Creative Genius

Caprice Lea

ISBN: 978-1-7354015-4-6 (paperback)

1st edition, April 2023

Printed in the United States of America

Those who tell the stories rule society.
— Plato

Reclaim your creative genius.
Create the life and community you desire.

For Sage and Kayli who continue to inspire me every day with their resilience, kindness, and creative genius.

Thank you Kayli for editing this book!

CONTENTS

Introduction

I was programmed to view myself and the world in a distorted way by school. Over past 25 years, I have deprogrammed my self and protected my daughters from being institutionalized like I was.

Our genius and creativity has been hidden from us. The good news is that these abilities are innate and just waiting for us to re-discover them. Welcome to this life-affirming journey!

I wrote *Instead of Schooling* in 2020 in response to the lockdowns that were happening in America. I realized that Americans would be less likely to passively submit to nonsense if they had not been schooled. Schooling has made obeying authority an unconscious reflex.

When I wrote *Instead of Schooling*, I focused on how school disrupts faculties of reason and harms our relationship with ourself. I highlighted the ways that these effects have taken over society. Since then, I've gained an even deeper understanding of the subject and that is what prompted me to write this book.

Many argue for education reform. However, I think focusing on fixing the system is nothing but a distraction from the fact that it was designed to break people. And when you look at the underbelly of schooling, you'll see just how intentional that is.

Schooling dumbs you down by focusing on rote memorization and drill-based exercises. It fills people with information that is not useful in real life. You are conditioned to bypass your reason and logic. You are forced to blindly accept what you are taught as truth. You are punished for coming to your own conclusions. Students are trained to just parrot back answers and regurgitate information to get a good grade or other meaningless, made-up rewards.

Over the course of the past three years, I've realized that almost everything we are taught in school is false. There's truth sprinkled in there, sure, but not as much as you'd think. I now realize that mostly everything we are taught about history, science, how the universe works, how the human body works is false. The reason for this is because the truth would make the whole system collapse.

The result of teaching false doctrines is that we believe our lives are an accident and the best we can do is to struggle for survival. This is the False Tapestry of Doom that has been sown into our minds to accept a disempowering and nihilistic worldview.

The good news is that once you pull on one thread of this tapestry, the entire thing falls apart.

To get people to passively comply with absurdity, you need to break their connection to the wisdom that they were born with — their inner knowing. You need to separate them physically and mentally from nature. Their brains need to be trained to passively absorb and regurgitate information so that their intelligence, curiosity, and imagination slowly go to sleep.

People need to believe they are somehow lacking and must compete for approval. You need to convince them that their self worth is connected to arbitrary scores and can only be determined by an outside authority. You need to train them to reflexively obey outside authorities, even if those authorities are not worth obeying.

It doesn't have to be this way. Most of us are born with a natural curiosity, imagination, desire to explore and play, and an innate sense of community with other people and animals. Believe it or not, most of us are born with creative genius.

In the 1960s, NASA funded a study to figure out how to recruit more geniuses. George Land led a research team that asked a very important question: What makes someone a genius? What they found was that 98% of 5 year-olds could be classified as a genius based on the use of their imagination to creatively solve problems. That's right, 98 percent! But by the time they were 10, only 30% were still connected to genius. When they reached 15, only 12% were geniuses. The reason that genius dropped from 98% to 12% in ten years? Schooling. Land then surveyed an adult population and found only 2% of adults were geniuses. Land attributed this to schooling and said that uncreative thinking and behavior is learned.

98% of us were born with creative genius. You create your world and life through your imagination. You can either use your imagination to recreate your past based on the way you were programmed by society. Or you can transform your life by reconnecting with your genius and imagination to create a beautiful, fulfilled life.

The process of schooling is toxic and the content of schooling is dangerous. If we didn't believe that the path to a well paying job requires K-12 schooling and then college, we would be free to pursue our unique path in life. A college degree is the big carrot and stick that keeps K-12 schooling frozen in place.

You might think that this can be corrected by reforming schooling. I already tried this path. There are powerful, wealthy controllers of society who have a strong vested interest in keeping schooling in place and making it even more soul crushing. Schooling was designed this way for a purpose and it is succeeding.

This books aims to provide an antidote. This is an invitation to unlearn school and then raise your sons and daughters in a way that preserves their genius.

The truth is that you can get into a great college without K-12 schooling and you can be happy and successful without a college degree. My family is proof of this. I home educated my oldest daughter K through 12 and she got a free ride to the college of her choice. She found it was a complete waste of time and is now building her own business. Remember, there is no standard path to happiness because happiness is an inner state of being.

One thing that you need to understand about me is that I will never ask you to replace one artificial belief system with another. Don't blindly believe anything I share. Investigate for yourself. Do the research. Take the time to explore through your direct experience.

I wrote this book to share what I have learned over the course of home educating my two daughters, getting $500,000 from the U.S. Department of Education to start two K-12 charter schools, cofounding a democratic Sudbury School, starting a self-directed learning center, creating a course on self-directed learning for the California Teachers College, and launching global learning and parent coaching programs for the selfDesign Learning Foundation. Welcome to the journey of deprogramming your mind and reconnecting to your genius!

I am honored that you are taking this journey with me. I am deeply indebted to all of the brilliant men and women that came before me who offered critiques of the institution of schooling and many insightful remedies including Brent Cameron, Joseph Chilton Pearce, Resa Steindel Brown, Ellen Hall, John Taylor Gatto, John Holt, Peter Gray, Maria Montessori, Ivan Illich, and many more.

Healing from School:
Essential Points

How you were programmed:

- Your brain was filled with random, biased information you were forced to memorize and repeat. Your mind was slowly disconnected from your intuition and inner knowing.

- Your natural state of unconditional love was replaced with fear and anxiety through operant conditioning (comparison, competition, sorting, grades, gold stars, public shaming).

- You were removed from nature and forced to sit still in an artificial, sterile, lifeless environment.

- Your ego was built up in the game of seeking (artificial grades, honor rolls, accolades) and suffering (bad grades, demerits, ridicule, and public shaming).

- Your heart was disconnected from your mind as you had to deny and repress uncomfortable feelings and sensations as you forced yourself to sit still.

- Your locus of control was moved from inner wisdom and knowing to an external authority.

Deprogramming your body-mind is simple and not easy:

- Your true nature is joy, peace, and contentment. Relax your mind and body. Be fully present, not thinking about the past or worrying about the future.

- Be aware and let it be.

- Live from your heart center and keep your heart open.

- Spend time in nature being fully present to life.

- Protect your mind from false beliefs, death-cult ideologies, and demons.

- Design a healing environment for you and your family. Set healthy boundaries, create loving relationships, play, laugh, grow your own food, do work that is meaningful and fulfilling.

- Learn how propaganda and mind control is used. Don't use any technology until you understand how it can be weaponized.

- Stand in truth. Don't participate in any lies.

- Embrace the unknown and let life guide you.

You are designed to learn, grow, and thrive in cooperation with life and your environment. True learning is natural and fun.

Beliefs are powerful. Young minds are plastic and moldable. They can be taught to believe anything.

Everything we are taught in school props up the war paradigm and benefits the people who control the bloated military industrial complex — the supranational corporation and international, private central banks.

Imagination is your creative genius. Imagine yourself to be who you want to be and your life to be full of love, goodness, beauty, and truth.

One:
The Toxic Cult of Schooling

It's not that I feel that school is a good idea gone wrong, but a wrong idea from the word go. It's a nutty notion that we can have a place where nothing but learning happens, cut off from the rest of life.

— John Holt

…without long-term confinement of children to great warehouses, the amount of isolation and mind-control needed to successfully introduce civil religion through schooling just wasn't available.

— John Taylor Gatto

We want one class of persons to have a liberal education, and we want another class of persons, a very much larger class, of necessity, in every society, to forego the privileges of a liberal education and fit themselves to perform specific difficult manual tasks.
— Woodrow Wilson, 1909, President of Princeton College

Schooling vs. Learning

Most people believe schooling is education. This drives the universal acceptance of forced government schooling. Most adults and parents that I speak with have never considered that there is an option other than school. School is viewed as the golden ticket to the good life.

This is a cultural myth that keeps us all trapped in an unnatural system of information processing and behavior control. I aim to show you that there are plenty of alternatives to schooling that preserve genius, expand human potential and goodness, and can be delivered affordably to all young men and women.

Education: a natural right to figure out who you are and what your place is in the world so that you can be fully responsible for your own life; pursuit of self-agency.

Learning: an innate capacity to adapt self to one's environment to grow and thrive. People are designed for active learning.

Schooling: society's attempt to control individuals by forcing them to be reflexively obedient to outside authorities. Schooling is designed around passive learning, rote memorization, and drill.

Controlling Minds with False Beliefs and Fear

Beliefs are super powerful. What we believe to be real and true was programmed into our minds before we knew how to protect our precious minds.

False beliefs are those that have no supporting evidence in nature or how life really works. When these ideas are put into practice, disharmony, chaos, and suffering ensue. The problem is that we have created a collective consensus of what is true based on false beliefs and carefully constructed myths.

I have come to realize that when I was taught false beliefs from such a young age in school, I didn't have the capacity to tell truth from fiction. I had no choice but to reflexively believe the lies I was taught. I did not have the power of reason or discernment as these stories were being planted in my mind.

We have never had an opportunity to challenge any of the theories or ideas that were fed to us in school. Now is the time to question everything.

Why is school so fear-based? I have come to realize that teachers are trapped in this negative environment where they rely on fear and shame to march kids through a curriculum that is neither interesting nor relevant to the real world.

Feeding Our Sons and Daughters to the Beast

Every story, myth, belief, and theory that we are taught in school serves to prop up the war paradigm and the military-industrial-biotech complex. The history lessons we are taught were written by the empire builders. The science lessons we are taught lead us to produce technology that harms life and living beings. The math we are taught dumbs us down. The way we are taught to read fosters illiteracy.

The military-industrial-biotech complex is set up to produce increasingly more sophisticated weapons. When you follow the money, it becomes clear that this agenda determines the content of school curriculum. Do we want our sons and daughters groomed to join the weaponry industry or help build a "livingry" industry as Buckminster Fuller calls it?

The underlying stories that we are told over and over during 18+ years of schooling slowly channel our gifts, talents, and creativity to serve our corporate masters. We are made to believe that we are passive victims of a fixed, external reality that exists without a purpose or a Creator. It is so hard to see this because we have been programmed with certain beliefs that seem so obvious to us, it is hard to understand that they are false beliefs. These myths keep us small, limited, and powerless.

What are these myths? One is that the universe is a random accident that happened when "The Big Bang" created something out of nothing billions of years ago. Ask yourself, using your power of reason, can something really come from nothing? Can life emerge from nothing? Absolutely not. If it could, then all of the scientists through the millennia would have figured out how to create life. They cannot create life from nothing.

We are forced in school to blindly believe everything that we are told and regurgitate this information on tests as if it is the one official "truth". Whether it is basic cell structure, the history of the United States, or the second law of thermodynamics, we are constantly told what to believe.

Other than mathematical proofs and dissections in biology class, we are offered no direct experience or experiment that would inform us if something was indeed true. This is passive learning of unverified myths and theories. Schools race to produce the most obedient and unimaginative human resources.

Why don't we view young men and women as precious souls with unique callings in life? Why aren't we educating them to be self-reliant and self-directed? Why does schooling take young men and women who are born geniuses and disconnect them from their genius and calling? Remember: 98% of 5 year olds are geniuses and only 2% of adults still have this connection to their genius.

What I discovered as I explored these questions was that schools were designed and forced upon society by men in the mid-1800s who put themselves above the rest of humanity in order to arrange and regulate people as if they were livestock. The cult of schooling has three legs: Humanism, Scientism, and Totalitarian Socialism.

Replacing God with the State: Religious Humanism

> *"If humanism were right in declaring that man is born to be happy, he would not be born to die. Since his body is doomed to die, his task on earth evidently must be of a more spiritual nature. It cannot be unrestrained enjoyment of everyday life. It cannot be the search for the best ways to obtain material goods and then cheerfully get the most out of them. It has to be the fulfillment of a permanent, earnest duty so that one's life journey may become an experience of moral growth, so that one may leave life a better human being then one started it."* — Aleksandr Solzhenitsyn

YOLO. You only live once. Therefore, it is perfectly okay to pursue the "unrestrained enjoyment of everyday life." Isn't that what we are sold by the media, advertisers, and our entertainment industry? Is it possible that this comes from Humanism? Yes indeed.

As Religious Humanists, the inventors of government schooling believed that there is no God, Creator, or Higher Power. In this worldview, the purposeless, random universe is slowly descending into a heat death. Humanists believe it is the duty and right of a superior group of men to become God-like and control the world in the absence of God.

John Dewey, the father of modern schooling, was a self-proclaimed Religious Humanist who worked to create a new religion based on the worldview of Humanism. Dewey was an author and one of 34 signers of the Humanist Manifesto I of 1933[1]. Important elements from this Manifesto include:

> *"Religious humanists regard the universe as self-existing and not created."*

> *"Humanism asserts that the nature of the universe depicted by modern science makes unacceptable any supernatural or cosmic guarantees of human values."*

> *"The distinction between the sacred and the secular can no longer be maintained."*

"Without theism or supernatural beliefs" is also a way of saying atheist. I firmly believe in the right for every individual to worship the God of their understanding, including believing there is no God."

The primary focus of Humanism is to exclude God, any higher power or creative force from society. Dewey said his goal was to create a humanist utopia and saw the school as the primary instrument of bringing forth this religion. John Dewey said that the teacher's calling is to be "the prophet of the true God and the usherer in of the true kingdom of God". When you realize that Dewey was a Marxist Humanist, you understand that he means "elite group of men" when he says "true God".

But is humanism really a religion? Yes it is. In 2014, the American Humanist Association claimed that Humanism is a religion and sued the United States to allow an inmate to create a humanist group in prison. Humanists won the motion in a U.S. District Court in Portland, Oregon.[2] "The court finds that Secular Humanism is a religion for Establishment Clause purposes." The court ruled that humanism should be treated as "religion" for purposes of the Equal Protection Clause, which prohibits religious discrimination.

I am not arguing for including religion in schools. The religion of Humanism is already being implicitly taught in schools. Humanism was defined by the United States as a religion. This religion has been taught in public schools for the past 150+ years. The Religious Humanists have re-branded themselves to just call it "Humanism" even though it is a religion.

I did my undergraduate studies at the University of Virginia, founded by Thomas Jefferson whose proudest achievement was the 1786 Virginia Statute for Religious Freedom. The separation of church and state as codified in the U.S. Constitution 1st Amendment is extremely important to protecting an individual's religious freedom:

Congress shall make no law respecting an establishment of religion, or prohibiting the free exercise thereof; or abridging the freedom of speech, or of the press; or the right of the people peaceably to assemble, and to petition the Government for a redress of grievances.

In the United States today[3], 70.6% of people describe themselves as Christian, 1.9% Jewish, 0.9% Buddhist, 0.7% Muslim, 0.7% Hindu, 3.1% atheist, 4% agnostic, and 15.8% "nothing in particular". Humanism fits into the atheist bucket. Notice that only 3.1% of Americans identify as atheists, yet this is the religion of the State and its institution of school.

Religious humanists believe that man, through the exercise of domination and control, can become like God. However, not all men could become God-like. The self-selected elite would play God and rule over the masses. This Master-Slave system was introduced by Aristotle in his work Politics written in 350 B.C. Aristotle didn't deny the soul, but he said that some men have the souls of masters and some of slaves.

It is clear, then, that some men are by nature free, and others slaves, and that for these latter slavery is both expedient and right. — Aristotle, Politics

The inventors of schooling took this view further and believed that men and women are soulless animals. Humanity is viewed as a herd — raw materials to be molded into workers and slaves. They chose to play God and be the molders of other people. Any wonder why corporations view men and women as "human resources"?

The men who invented compulsory schooling used the power of government to force all children to attend the schools that they invented. The inventors of schooling tested these inhumane practices in public schools in India and the Soviet Union before using taxpayer money to fund their artificial institutions in America.

Horace Mann was largely responsible for getting the first state schools legislated in Massachusetts. He travelled the state giving impassioned speeches saying that parents are not capable of educating their children. Ironically, he chose to homeschool his three sons. This hypocrisy is continued today by the wealthy who could afford to move into the best public school districts but opt for small private technology-free schools for their sons and daughters instead⁴.

It is one thing for a man or group of men to decide that a school of their invention would benefit some children. They have a right to their ideas. And they have a right to employ their own resources to create these schools and invite families to pay for these schools. But they created these indoctrination camps only for the "lower classes".

The effect of schools teaching humanism is that people have lost their moral compass and feel that life is meaningless. They are encouraged to pursue pleasure without restraint. You need only look at the degradation of our culture and the ugliness in music, art, architecture, film and television programming to see that we have lost our way.

Several false theories proceed from Humanism: the main one is the idea that life emerged from nothing and is evolving randomly, by chance. Generations of individuals believe that they are alone in a cold, uncaring universe. Scientific advances in quantum physics, quantum biology and consciousness studies are systematically excluded from K-12 curriculum.

If you take God/Creator/Higher Power/Universal Intelligence out of society, isn't there a huge void? Won't we just descend into anarchy and chaos? This is where the religion of Scientism steps in.

Humanism couldn't succeed without its sister religion Scientism. When you take God out of the picture, you need something else to worship. The elite controllers believed that science, through the use of technology, can control nature and men can become like God.

Debunking Scientism

I love science. I'm scared of scientism because I see that there is a strong movement to create a scientific dictatorship using the shield of "public health". Public health is a weapon in the hands of a psychopathic elite once you really understand how the body works and how we really get sick, which we explore later in this book.

If you haven't watched Rupert Sheldrake's banned TED talk, The Science Delusion5, I highly recommend it. The science delusion is the false belief that science has figured everything out and just needs to work out the details.

Sheldrake points out the difference between science as a method of inquiry based on reason, evidence, hypothesis and collective investigation and science as a belief system or worldview. He states that science as a belief system restricts the free inquiry of science. Sheldrake points out that science has been taken over by the belief in materialism, which is the belief that only matter exists. This serves to deny our direct experience of our consciousness.

Scientism is the belief that science can provide all the answers and solutions. If science could do this, would we be in such dire straits? In Sheldrake's book, Science Set Free, and in his TEDx6talk he debunks the ten dogmas of science:

1. Nature is mechanical. (This includes your body.)
2. Matter is unconscious. (Including plants, trees, animals, humans.)
3. The Laws of Nature are fixed.
4. Nature is purposeless.
5. The amount of energy and matter is fixed.
6. Biological inheritance is only material, through genes.
7. Memories are stored in the brain.
8. Your mind is in your brain.
9. Non-local mind activity (telekinesis, remote viewing, etc.) are just illusions.
10. Mechanistic medicine is the only effective approach.

All of these dogmas are taught in school as if they are true.

Contemporary science is based on the claim that all reality is material or physical. There is no reality but material reality. Consciousness is a by-product of the physical activity of the brain. Matter is unconscious. Evolution is purposeless. God exists only as an idea in human minds, and hence in human heads.

*These beliefs are powerful, not because most scientists think about them critically but because they **don't**.*

— Rupert Sheldrake, Science Set Free

Dogma #8 is particularly harmful and leads to the mechanistic training of brains. By limiting the mind to the computer-like brain, materialists deny the existence of human creativity.

Many people think the mind is contained within the brain, that it is a product of the brain. But how can this be true when the mind processes meaning, whereas we have already shown that the brain is a computing machine that cannot originate meaning?

— Amit Goswami, The Everything Answer Book

Rather than having a blind trust in Scientism, we need to challenge existing paradigms that seem to be marching us off a cliff. You will not find any school in the country challenging the false dogmas on which Scientism is based.

The Malthusian Myth

*The power of population is so superior to the power in the earth to produce subsistence for man, that premature death must in some shape or other visit the human race…We should facilitate, instead of foolishly and vainly endeavoring to impede, the operations of nature in producing this mortality… **In our towns we should make the streets narrower, crowd more people into the houses, and court the return of the plague.***

— Thomas Malthus

Thomas Malthus was not a scientist, but a manager at the British East India Company. Malthus was a strong proponent of limiting and controlling the human population. Malthusians used (possibly mis-used) the ideas of Charles Darwin to support social Darwinism and eugenics. But Darwin's theory of evolution is a theory with no supporting evidence.

There has never been one fossil found that provides evidence for one species to evolve into a new species. Yes, species adapt to their environment over time. But they do not evolve into a completely new species. Not even life as simple as bacteria have been found to evolve into another species of bacteria. Secular scientists have also discovered that mutations within species are not random[7].

Social darwinism and its distortion of the *theory* of evolution justifies the oligarchs' desire to mold the global population into two classes: an elite ruling class and a mass of workers and debt slaves. Evolution has no scientific basis. The theory was created to justify eugenics - the culling of the population to create a superior species.

According to the National Women's Law Center, 17 states in the United States have laws that allow the permanent, forced sterilization of children with disabilities. Some of these laws were passed as recently as 2019. Forced sterilization is part of the eugenics movement that became unthinkable after WWII. Prior to that, forced sterilization of black women in the south was so common, it was sometimes called a "Mississippi Appendectomy".

Even John Maynard Keynes, one the most influential economists of the 20th century was a neo-Malthusian.

> *We of this society are neo-Malthusians... I believe that for the future the problem of population will emerge in the much greater problem of Hereditary and Eugenics. Quality must become the preoccupation. — John Maynard Keynes*

Keynes, is speaking of the "quality" of the human population, which neo-Malthusians feel entitled to control. The false dialectic of free markets vs. centralized economy offers only two predetermined possibilities for organizing the economy, which is ridiculous. I am indebted to Matthew Ehret's excellent research on this topic and point you to his CanadianPatriot.org[8] website.

In America, there was a strong anti-Malthusian movement that has been forgotten. Benjamin Franklin, Abraham Lincoln, and John F. Kennedy were all against the destructive ideas of the Malthusian Law of Population. Kennedy lost his battle against the empire builders who strove to enslave humanity.

> *Malthus argued a century and a half ago that man, by using up all his available resources, would forever press on the limits of subsistence, thus condemning humanity to an indefinite future of misery and poverty. We can now begin to hope and, I believe, know that Malthus was expressing not a law of nature, but merely the limitation then of scientific and social wisdom.*

— *President John F. Kennedy*[9]

Scientism and Humanism work together to convince men and women that the world is a random accident without a Creator and that man, though the use of science and technology can create a Utopian society where the masses are controlled with bread and circuses. Here is where the third leg of schooling — totalitarian socialism/communism and technocracy — play their part.

School as a Weapon of Totalitarian Socialism/Communism

Do you ever wonder why so many young men and women think that socialism is a good idea? Even though over 200 million innocent men and women have been murdered in the name of socialism[10] and every attempt to create a socialist society has ended in utter failure and extreme poverty?

To explain socialism in a nutshell, imagine that you are taking a college class. The instructor tells the class that everyone will get a C no matter how much they work or what the quality of their work is.

Who is going to want to work? Nobody! And the University still gets all of your tuition even if you are not learning anything.

The men who invented and championed forced government schooling in the 19th and 20th Centuries knew exactly what they were doing. They believed that human nature was corrupt, that life is random - not a gift from a higher power, and that they could create a Utopian society by controlling people.

The totalitarian communist Leon Trotsky (a Soviet communist revolutionary) revered the father of modern American schools, John Dewey. The way that schools were described in the Soviet Union in the early 1900s is almost identical to how they are described in the United States today.

John Dewey wrote: "The mere absorbing of facts and truths is so exclusively individual an affair that it tends very naturally to pass into selfishness. There is no obvious social motive for the acquirement of mere learning, there is no clear social gain in success thereat." [11]

Marxist Socialists have the goal of creating a Utopia similar to what you read about in George Orwell's 1984. In this world, men and women are controlled and have no desires, calling, or connection to God. The thing is that there is no such thing as Utopia. Empathy comes from acknowledging death and celebrating life. Empathy is the opposite of utopia and, along with a conscience, it what defines humanity.

Most humans are empathic beings. The exception being those who have a dark-triad personality disorder (narcissistic, anti-social, borderline) or psychopathy. When the men in the 1800s set out to create a utopian society, they designed it from the distorted filter of their dystopian beliefs. They lacked empathy and a conscience.

Critical Race Theory: Marxism Repackaged

The purpose of cultural Marxism is to divide society into groups of victims and oppressors and pit them against each other. People are so focused on their victim story and getting back at the oppressors, that they fail to realize that most of us are enslaved by the masters that control the supranational corporations and central banks which print money out of thin air.

If people of all skin colors, socio-economic conditions, education levels, and belief systems came together demanding that the parasitic class who control money and industry returned our assets, money, and life energy to us, the game would shift instantly.

Have injustices been perpetuated? Absolutely. Are black men incarcerated at a higher proportion than other groups. Yes. Many men and women struggle to support their families and survive. It is easy to emotionally manipulate people who know that the economy is rigged and want to punish someone.

The largest teacher's union in the country, the National Education Association is highly political and aims to sow division through identity politics. To confirm this, read the NEA's 2022-23 Resolutions on the website, which take a highly politicized stance on everything from immigration, abortion, health care, and overthrowing the white supremacy culture. Here's an excerpt:

> *"The National Education Association believes that, in order to achieve racial and social justice, educators must acknowledge the existence of White supremacy culture as a primary root cause of institutional racism, structural racism, and White privilege.[12]"*

The NEA has a political agenda and is the union for 3.2 million public school teachers in the United States. There is indeed a war for the minds of young men and women by first attacking the minds of teachers.

A solid education in the history of empire, the Federal Reserve system, fiat currency, and natural law will facilitate productive conversations and generate workable solutions. We can opt out of the war paradigm and refuse to fund wars. First we need to stop warring with each other. Then we put the parasites to work in jobs that actually contribute something to society.

Technocracy Today

It is helpful to know what the oligarchs have planned for us. They have been working for 150 years to prepare us for a dystopian future similar to that in George Orwell's 1984.

> *In sum, Technocracy subsumes Scientism as a religion where technocrats represent the priesthood that worships the god of Science and Technology… Scientism is at the root of both Technocracy and Transhumanism, indicating that the revolution waged against the world is religious in nature. Historically, all religious wars were ultimately ended by sheer force and total domination.*
>
> — *Technocracy News and Trends*[13]

As we witness the oligarchy embracing technocracy and transhumanism, it seems like humanism and scientism run amok. The bankster oligarchs are now trying to replace God with the Silicon Valley boys. A few quotes from World Economic Forum advisor, Noah Yuval Harari:

> *If you have enough data, and you have enough computing power, you can understand people better than they understand themselves and then you can manipulate them in ways that were previously impossible and in such a situation, the old democratic systems stop functioning. We need to re-invent democracy in this new era in which humans are now hackable animals. The whole idea that humans have this 'soul' or 'spirit' and have free will… that's over.*[14]

> *I think the biggest question in economics and politics in the coming decades will be 'what to do with all these useless people?' I don't think we have an economic model for that… the problem is more boredom and what to do with them and how will they find some sense of meaning in life when they*

are basically meaningless, worthless? My best guess at
present, is a combination of drugs and computer games.

Matthew Ehret does a beautiful job of framing the two competing paradigms that are battling for our minds. The first paradigm is a dead, soulless universe without a Creator that is spiraling toward heat destruction and must be controlled through technocracy and transhumanism. This worldview emerges from the second law of thermodynamics: entropy which claims that the universe will devolve into a "heat death". However, entropy is widely misunderstood. It was a theory that started as a thought experiment and has not been validated by studying living systems. Entropy only works for a situation of equilibrium or stillness. Nature is never still.

Thermodynamics therefore deals only with situations of
stillness. Time plays no role in it. In reality, of course, nature
never stands still, and time does matter. Everything is in a
constant state of flux. The fact that classical thermodynamics
is limited to equilibrium situations may come as a surprise...
the second law does not mandate a steady degeneration. It
quite happily coexists with the spontaneous development of
order and complexity.

— J. Miguel Rubí[15]

The second paradigm is based on a benevolent, loving Creator who endowed men and women with reason, imagination, and creativity. In this paradigm, men and women model their governance systems after Natural Laws that favor diversity, creativity, and cooperation. Note I am not saying "government". There is a huge difference between government as an institution and governance as a process.

Which paradigm do you prefer to live under? I prefer to love God, protect and preserve the beautiful paradise that we are heirs to, follow the Golden Rule, and give freely of my gifts and talents as we build a more beautiful world.

The Elite Families Fund Public Schools

Forced compulsory schooling did not come about because parents didn't want to educate their children or couldn't so so. It was a planned and well funded initiative that was forced on Americans to warp young men and women's minds. The elites wanted to alienate young men and women from their families and God.

The takeover of American education was a critical piece in the plan to create a new world order based on humanism, scientism, and totalitarian socialism/communism.

> *In 1889, William Torrey Harris, the U.S. Commissioner of Education, told a high-ranking railroad official that the schools were being scientifically designed not to overeducate children. He believed that the schools **should** alienate children from their parents and religion. In 1890, Carnegie wrote eleven essays which were published under the title The Gospel of Wealth. **The underlying premise was that the free-enterprise system had been locked-up by men such as himself, J.P. Morgan, and John D. Rockefeller, and that they not only owned everything, but also controlled the government. His worry, was that subsequent generations would realize this, and work against them. His solution was to control the education system,** and to create a direct relationship between the amount of education a person had, and how good of a job they could get. Therefore, this created a motivation for children to attend school, where they would be taught only what the social engineers of this country wanted them to know.*

> — *David Allen Rivera, Final Warning: A History of the New World Order*[16]

State Schools Were Actively Opposed by Americans

There is a myth that schooling is a positive and necessary institution at the center of American culture. This ignores the fact that Americans actively opposed forced governmental schooling and young men and women were often marched to public school at gunpoint.

Ellwood Cubberley, an early expert in school administration, helped create one of the first schools of education at Stanford and legitimized "education" as a field of study. Cubberley tells us, "The history of compulsory-attendance legislation in the states has been much the same everywhere, and everywhere laws have been enacted only after overcoming strenuous opposition."

The coercion required to keep young men and women sitting quietly in their seats as teachers march them through boring, standardized curriculum breaks their spirits. It is breaking the spirits of teachers too.

Schooling is a terrible misuse of government power. I do realize that government schools are, for some children, the safest place for them to be. I don't think dismantling schools today is the answer for all children. And let's be honest about what schooling really is. Schooling is a completely made-up, unnatural way of trying to force children to comply with a strange set of rules. Every child deserves an education that preserves genius.

Schooling continues because there are state laws that make it illegal not to school your child. The force of government keeps it in place. Compulsory schooling hides under the banner of improving people and society even though it continues to produce ignorant, illiterate people and research shows that schooling perpetuates socio-economic inequality.

The Trouble with Moral Relativism

You may not yet be alarmed by the teaching of Humanism, Scientism, or Socialism in school. What these doctrines do is state that, since there is no God or higher power, there is no Absolute Truth. In the absence of absolute truth, everyone is free to decide what is true and false.

If there is no higher power, then we are not accountable to God for our behavior. Morals are relative. It depends on the situation if an action is right or wrong. Life on earth becomes not just a survival of the fittest, but a playground for unbridled pursuit of pleasure. You only live once has become the mantra of the younger generations.

We are told that Science will provide us with all of the answers. Scientism denies the existence of our inner subjective world of experience. It focuses on the "external world" as if it is a fixed reality that we have no affect over.

We are witnessing a society in which hedonistic pleasure and ego pursuits have replaced the old-fashioned virtues of temperance, patience, charity, and service to others.

School is Working Perfectly

Trying to reform schools so that they educate people is impossible because the very design of school is designed to impede learning and the development of self-agency so that people can be controlled. Read that again. Designed to impede the development of self-agency. The wealthy and powerful in this country still don't send their children to public school.

Schooling damages people and limits their views of themselves. School creates within people a deep sense of insecurity and fear. Endless comparisons, competition, grades and testing are inhumane and teach people that their self-worth can be shown on a bell curve. The school system has nothing to do with real, lasting learning. Rather than educating and empowering people, schooling breaks human spirits and creates fearful, dependent people who cannot separate fact from fiction.

Schooled People Maintain the Status Quo

Students in K-12 schooling and college make few cognitive gains, aren't learning useful life skills, and aren't enjoying the process, so why do we force them to spend the first 24 years of their lives in school? Schooling produces the people who maintain the status quo and prop up our growth-driven consumer economy. Schooled people will work at mundane jobs for low wages and consume all the stuff that our economy needs to sell to survive. It was designed this way.

Am I the only one who sees the extreme foolishness of this business of breaking children's spirits with the belief that there is a body of knowledge they need to memorize? The harm of using arbitrary, subjective grades to determine the value of a person? The foolishness of putting them in a collectivistic environment that forces them to compete as individuals all doing the same boring, meaningless tasks. It's all completely absurd. People are suffering because their souls have been schooled and their minds have been institutionalized.

Two:
The Failure Industry

Commerce is supported by keeping the individual at odds with himself and others, by making us want more than we need, and offering credit to buy what refined senses do not want.

The masses become shackled; I see how their eyes weep and are desperate — of course they feel desperate — for something, for some remedy

That a poor soul then feels needs to be bought.

I find nothing more offensive than a god who could condemn human instincts in us that time in all its wonder have made perfect.

I find nothing more destructive to the well-being of life than to support a god that makes you feel unworthy and in debt to it. I imagine erecting churches to such a strange god will assure endless wars that commerce loves.

A god that could frighten is not a god — but an insidious idea and a weapon in the hands of the insane. A god who talks of sin is worshipped by the infirm;

I was once spiritually ill — we all pass through that — but one day the intelligence in my soul cured me.

— Meister Eckhart (1260-1328), An Insidious Idol

Why Government Schooling is "Free"

Schooling is paid for by taxpayer dollars so of course it's not really "free" because the government doesn't create or produce anything and has no source of income other than taxes. I had the honor of taking an economics class with Nobel Prize winning economist Herbert Simon, who told our class "the only job of the government is to redistribute wealth".

Schooling is free for the same reason that social media is free. Men and women are the products. Schooling deprograms happy, peaceful, cooperative, altruistic creators and programs them to be insecure, fearful, competitive, passive consumers. Aren't you grateful that these deprogramming-reprogramming camps are free? What are the hidden costs of schooling? Our happiness and creativity.

College Doesn't Offer Everyone a Positive ROI

The belief that getting into a good college will guarantee you a job and financial security is misguided. 25% of recent college graduates are unemployed and have an average of $27,000 in college loan debt. 70% of graduates from half of the colleges in the U.S. make less than high school graduates[17]. Let that sink in. Read the source data.

Yet college tuition has risen 1200% since 1978, and the average college grad has $30,000 in student debt with monthly payments of $393. 45% of people with student loans don't think college was worth it[18] and 36% of college graduates had no cognitive gains after 4 years of college. Young people are bored, anxious, depressed, not learning much, and college becomes indentured servitude for many people.

Student loan debt will only be forgiven if they work for 5 years for the government, a non-profit, or an education institution. What a scam! Really? Why would a bankruptcy court forgive the credit card debt that you used to buy a flat-screen TV but not the Fannie Mae loan you got to pay for your college education? College and university tuition rates have skyrocketed in correlation to the ease of getting student loans.

In my initial research on ROI, I have found that 40% of liberal arts majors are working in jobs that don't require a degree. It's not necessarily true that STEM careers are the way to go. On average, those who pursue TEM (technology, engineering, maths) education and careers have a positive ROI on their college tuition. S degrees (biology, zoology, geology, etc.) do worse than some social science and English majors. Social science majors often fare well in the long-term because they get advanced degrees. However, I have many friends with mounds of debt from this strategy.

By now you might be thinking, "Okay Caprice, it's fine if you want to risk your daughters' futures by telling them that they don't need to go to college. But, I'm certainly not that stupid." Here is what I say to my daughters, "If on your chosen path, it makes sense for you to go to college, I will support you and help make it happen."

The trouble is most of the stuff that kids learn in college doesn't prepare them for a successful life or career. And usually, college graduates focus on getting good paying jobs to pay off their new student loans. So, most college graduates cannot even follow their callings, if they were lucky enough to discover them while spending 7+ hours a day at school.

I had a double major in cultural anthropology and international relations at University of Virginia then got an MBA in finance at Carnegie Mellon. I was told that liberal arts was the way to go because it teaches you to think. I was told that college isn't about getting a job or contributing to the economy. It's about expanding your intellectual capacity and expanding your horizons.

Well, maybe that was true in the 1980s and 1990s before the widespread availability of the internet, free online college courses, YouTube, and coding schools. Today you can learn anything online. I can think of thousands of more affordable ways to increase your intellectual capacity, broaden your horizons, and build concrete skills than going to college. And they can all be self-directed by each individual according to her learning style, interests, and optimal pace of learning.

K-12 schools point to college as if it is a requirement for a successful career or a fulfilling life. Parents are fed fear-based myths about what will happen to their children if they don't go to college. Much of this is funded by sophisticated marketing and PR campaigns.

Debunking the School-Job-Happiness Myth

My youngest daughter said to me when she was 12 years old and trying out public school to make friends in our new town:

> *Mom, have you noticed that school is designed so that kids in elementary school are learning what they need to get into middle school? Middle school kids are learning what they need for high school. And high school kids are learning what they need to pass tests and get into college. That doesn't make any sense. It's all telling us that we are just preparing for a future that never quite gets here. That's stupid.*

We submit to schooling because there is a strong bias against people who don't have a college degree and we have been fed the myth that this is the path to happiness.

The School-Job-Happiness Myth is deeply flawed and destructive to many generations. Even if education does lead you to a high-paying job... Who says that you will be happy?

In my work as an executive coach, many of my clients have been adults in their 30s, 40s, and 50s who were well paid in the corporate world and struggling to find meaning, purpose and joy in their lives. I also don't think that most people want to work only 4 hours a week and lounge on the beach. This might be cool for a few months, but then our natural desire to be connected to a higher purpose kicks in.

And there is a parallel in corporate American today. Gallup's State of the American Workplace survey finds that only 13% of adults are "engaged" at work - they look forward to it and believe it is meaningful. The rest are sleepwalking through their workday, waiting for the weekend (63%) or they hate it (24%).

Johann Hari, author of *Lost Connections: Uncovering the Real Causes of Depression – and the Unexpected Solutions,* found that people who don't believe their work is meaningful and feel they have no control over their time and activities in their workplace are more likely to be depressed and stressed. He recommends focusing on the power imbalances in the workplace rather than a theoretical chemical brain imbalance in individuals. Perhaps we should consider the power imbalance in K-12 schools?

The Taboo Against the Self-Educated

Even though 56% of American adults don't think college is worth it[19], most entry level jobs still require a college degree. College is more about credentialing and indoctrination, not learning.

Many parents live in fear that their children won't get into a "top" university and therefore never have a good chance at success and riches. So they focus on grades and often over-schedule their children with extracurricular activities to make sure that their kids can get into a prestigious college.

College is best approached as part of a larger plan. It is an expensive proposition to hope that a person will discover her gifts and talents at university. A few do. Most don't.

Bryan Caplan, an economist and author of The Case Against Education says that a college degree is mainly a signaling device of employability because you don't get any social creds for doing one or two years. He makes a good case.

"Education is a waste of time and money because so much of the payoff for education isn't really coming from learning useful job skills. Nor is it coming from students savoring the educational experience. Rather, most of what's going on is that people are showing off — or, as economists call it, they are 'signaling'. They are trying to impress future employers by showing how dedicated they are." – Bryan Caplan

If children aren't gaining useful skills and aren't enjoying the process, then why do we force them to spend the first 24 years of your life in school? These are the years when humans have the most energy, creativity, and imagination. Until it is schooled out of them.

If college admissions looked different, then K-12 schooling would most likely have different standards. High schools across the country added Algebra and Geometry as a graduation requirement after Harvard made these courses an entry requirement. The powerful University of California system has a list of required A-G high school classes that one must pass to attend a UC school. K-12 schooling is currently designed to transmit inert knowledge so that students get good scores on tests and the SAT/ACT.

The Failure Industry

School is failing most young people. In the 2015 & 2016 Gallup Student Polls of students in grades 5-12[20]:

- 67% of high school seniors are "not engaged/actively disengaged" in school

- 50% of students in grades 5-12 are "not engaged/actively disengaged" in school.

- 52% feel stuck or discouraged.

This failed schooling industry is making big money. There are 50.8 million youth in public elementary, middle, and high schools. There were 19.9 million students attending a college or university in fall 2019. That's a big, captive audience for edTech companies, textbook manufacturers, and testing companies.

Schooling in the United States is a $1.3 trillion industry. $1,350,000,000,000. There are a lot of companies making a lot of money – including textbook manufacturers, standardized testing companies, and EdTech startups. Schooling advocates have powerful lobbying interests that keep schooling funded and prevent alternatives from emerging. Schooling is an education monopoly.

$13,440 is spent per student for public K-12 school each year on average for a total of $680 billion every year. Americans spent $80 billion just on back-to-school purchases in 2019. Philanthropy to support public education is over $60 billion a year.

The results of public schooling are shockingly grim, evidenced by the high illiteracy rates among 15-year olds[21], college graduates[22], and adults[23]; lack of engagement[24]; student boredom[25]; skyrocketing anxiety, depression, and suicide; continued teacher turnover, and widespread ignorance of fundamental knowledge.

> *Over the past decade, there has been no progress in either mathematics or reading performance, and the lowest-performing students are doing worse. In fact, over the long term in reading, the lowest-performing students—those readers who struggle the most—have made no progress from the first NAEP administration almost 30 years ago.*
>
> *— Peggy Carr, Associate Commissioner of the National Center for Education Statistics, which administers the National Assessment of Educational Progress (NAEP)[26]*

What is clear is that almost 55 years of federal education policy has not resulted in student success in reading and math. What has this focus on national standards and testing done for students and teachers? Teachers who enter schooling because they love a subject or love kids, judge themselves harshly when the kids are not engaged or acting out. Often, they feel like it is a personal failure, or they see the inertia in the system and leave. More than 41% of teachers leave the profession within five years of starting.[27]

Homeschooling Under Attack

Even though public schools are ineffective at teaching reading, math, and civics, the NEA believes that parents cannot provide a "comprehensive education experience". The National Education

Association, that claims to have 3.2 million teachers as members, states in its 2022-23 Resolutions:

> *The National Education Association believes that home schooling programs based on parental choice cannot provide the student with a comprehensive education experience. When home schooling occurs, students enrolled must meet all state curricular requirements, including the taking and passing of assessments to ensure adequate academic progress. Home schooling should be limited to the children of the immediate family, with all expenses being borne by the parents/guardians. Instruction should be by persons who are licensed by the appropriate state education licensure agency, and a curriculum approved by the state department of education should be used.*

> *The Association also believes that home-schooled students should not participate in any extracurricular activities in the public schools.*

> *The Association further believes that local public school systems should have the authority to determine grade placement and/or credits earned toward graduation for students entering or re-entering the public school setting from a home school setting. (1988, 2006)*

A study by Dr. Lawrence Rudner of 20,760 homeschooled students, called Strengths of Their Own, found the homeschoolers who have homeschooled all their school aged years had the highest academic achievement. This was especially apparent in the higher grades. Another important finding of was that the race of the student does not make any difference. There was no significant difference between minority and white homeschooled students. These findings show that when parents, regardless of race, commit themselves to make the necessary sacrifices and tutor their children at home, almost all obstacles present in other school systems disappear.

Homeschooling continues to be under attack around the world. The attacks come by making it illegal to homeschool, placing strict regulations on homeschooling, and bribing families with money to homeschool under a government umbrella. It is obvious that the State doesn't want you to educate your sons and daughters in the private

Breaking the Trance

Everyone admits that the school system is broken and yet parents still support public school. Schooling occupies a central position in American society. The shared social belief is that schooling is good for everyone and necessary for democracy and economic equality. Most adults cannot conceive of their lives functioning if their children aren't being cared for by the institution of school. Why is this?

Rational irrationality, confirmation bias, and motivated ignorance help explain why schooling is still supported.

Economist Bryan Caplan's concept of "rational irrationality" helps to explain this phenomenon. If you believe that you cannot change a situation (schooling), you will not accept evidence (kids hate school and aren't learning much) that refutes your cherished belief (school is good) because the emotional cost is too high. Most people do not think that they personally can do anything about the school system, so they refute any evidence that shows how damaging it is for young men and women.

Confirmation bias will lead people to focus on one amazing teacher or the one child that "seems to" love school. I have always been curious why a parent's perspective is often so different than their child's own experience of school. Many children have told my daughters over the years that they dislike school and wish they could homeschool too. When I speak with the children's mothers, they universally tell me that their child likes school and their school is the best in the community.

Motivated ignorance is when we choose not to know more, we actively choose not to understand. We have developed a conception of the world and willfully remain ignorant to avoid cognitive dissonance which occurs when we hold two opposing ideas in our minds. Motivated ignorance makes us more confident in our belief systems and less likely to consider facts that contradict our beliefs.

If someone raises an objection to government schooling or proposes an alternative, school supporters will raise the question of what the objector has to gain and question the person's motives. School supporters will also require impossibly high standards for proposed education alternatives while relaxing the standard for research supporting government schooling.

We have the school system that we think we deserve. Rational irrationality, confirmation bias, and motivated ignorance combine to make the majority of people blind to the ills and abuses of forced government schooling.

Educating yourself is a human right that should be protected in a republic that was formed under God's Laws. People don't see this as a right because they mistakenly think that schooling is education. Compulsory schooling is producing people who feel broken and unworthy because it denies the existence of our soul and your soul's calling.

Schooling writes our story for us and then deposits us into it.

Three: The War for Your Mind

*I think the subject that will be of the most importance politically, is mass psychology. Its importance has been enormously increased by the growth of modern methods of propaganda of these the most influential is what is called education. Religion plays a part though a diminishing one, the press the cinema and the radio play an increasing part. **It maybe hoped that in time anybody will be able to persuade anybody of anything**, if you can catch the patient young, and is provided by the state with money and equipment. The subject will make great strides when it's taken up by scientists under a **scientific dictatorship**. The social psychologists of the future will have a number of classes of school children in whom they will try different methods of producing an **unshakable conviction that snow is black**. Various results will soon be arrived at that:*

1. *the influence of home is obstructive (destruction of the family unit)*
2. *not much can be done unless indoctrination begins before the age of ten*
3. *verses set to music and repeatedly intoned are very effective*

*4. opinion that snow is white must be held to show a morbid taste for eccentricity but I anticipate its for the future scientists to make these maxims precise and **discover how much it costs per head to make children believe snow is black and how much less it would cost for them to believe snow is dark grey**.*

*Although the science will be diligently studied it will be rigidly confined to the governing class. **The populace will not be allowed to know how their convictions were generated.** Every government thats been in charge of education for a generation will be able to control its subjects securely without the need for armies of policeman."*

— Lord Bertrand Russell, Impact of Science on Society

Your Mind is Private

Self knowledge is the highest knowing. Your inner voice and intuition are your guiding forces. Your mind should be private. It is your connection to God.

The power of your mind and imagination is blocked in schooling through operant conditioning, drill, and rote memorization. We are never guided to understand how our mind, creativity and imagination work. Instead we are taught to value our intellect over our innate intelligence.

An important distinction is to make is the difference between your brain and your mind.

> *The nature of the mind is the most unsolved problem that science cannot deal with. It cannot deal with the fact that we are conscious, and our thoughts and experiences don't seem to be inside your brain.*
>
> *— Rupert Sheldrake*

Your mind extends beyond your brain. Some scientists who study consciousness look at the brain as a receiver of information, not as a generator or storage device. We have a lot to discover about how our mind works. I invite you to explore the nature of your experience and where your thoughts and greatest ideas come from.

I posit that intelligence is innate and the intellect (or brain) is programmed with information. It is helpful to know how to get home, bake cookies, change a tire, etc. But your intellect is not a good tool for self-knowledge or creative endeavors.

Our intellect is merely a computer-like tool that our minds can use. We cannot get anything out of our brains except the information that we put into it. Scientists are exploring where memory is stored and some interesting theories are that memories are stored in water (the interstitial fluid in our body) or that morphogenic fields store thoughts and memories.

Schools as Psych Labs

School today is more like a psychology lab and less like an institution of learning. And the psychological tools that are being used as weapons against our sons and daughters are powerful.

Schools are the greatest weapons that are used against our minds, imaginations, and creativity. In the late 1800's psychologists starting thinking about what kind of children they could mold to fit their totalitarian utopian vision. The started worrying less about what was taught in school and began working on how to mold children.

William Wundt was an experimental psychologist who viewed human beings as just bodies with brains and nervous systems. In this view, there are no souls or free will and actions are predetermined. The job of the psychologist is to condition a child to get desired behaviors. Wundt's work inspired Pavlov, Watson, and Skinner whose experiments all trickled into the classroom.

> *Few Americans know that almost every development in psychology in the United States in the past sixty-five years has been directed by the Bureau of Psychological Warfare of the British Army. A short time ago, the present writer learned a new name, The Tavistock Institute of London, also known as the Tavistock Institute of Human Relations. Human relations covers every aspect of human behavior, and it is the modest goal of the Tavistock institute to obtain and exercise control over every aspect of human behavior of American citizens.*

> *— Eustace Mullins, Secrets of the Federal Reserve[28]*

The command center for the psychological conditioning and mind control of Americans has been the Tavistock Institute, which has been dedicated to the degradation of American culture. It is still quite active today. Look around and ask yourself if our culture (music, art, architecture, film, and television programming) are beautiful or ugly? Are we being asked to believe that ugly is beautiful?

The Sham of BioPsychiatry

When we experience psychological suffering or don't automatically comply to external demands, we are labeled with ADHD, depression, mood disorders, etc. We are told that we have a genetic disposition for this or a chemical imbalance in our brains. This is all made up nonsense.

Most of psychiatry is a scam and has no scientific basis for its treatments or methods.[29] All of the "diagnoses" contained in the 1,050 page Diagnostic and Statistical Manual of Mental Disorders (DSM-V) were invented and voted on by committee. There is nothing scientific about these diagnoses. If you don't believe me, watch the excellent documentary, Diagnostic and Statistical Manual: Psychiatry's Deadliest Scam[30].

Ty Colbert, PhD, author of The Four False Pillars of Biopsychiatry, goes through all of the research on schizophrenia and shows that there is no evidence for the current disease model of "mental illness". He proves that they have never found a gene or group of genes responsible for mental illness, there is no evidence that it is inherited, there is no evidence that there exists chemical imbalances.

What could be causing any of the brain differences seen in MRIs? Stress and traumatic experiences. Are young men and women stressed in school? Is school traumatic for many people? Yes indeed.

When someone is under stress, more cortisol is secreted into the brain tissue area than is secreted under normal circumstances. As a result, the brain loses some of its ability to absorb water. The brain shrinks slightly because it is holding less water, not because it is affected by some biological disease.

— Ty Colbert, PhD

Also, commonly used drugs like Ritalin and Prozac are toxic to the brain. The brain creates a protective mechanism to protect it from these toxic drugs. This might look like relief in the short term, but in the longer term, the brain is damaged. The conclusion? We should not look to medication to cure or manage a non-existent disease[31].

Rather than medicating our young men and women, we need to ensure that their lives are as stress-free as possible and that the learning environment is focused on love and well-being.

Gender Confusion

There is an insane movement to replace "mother" with "birth parent". It doesn't get any more anti-life or anti-woman than that! The mother archetype is one of the most important archetypes in society. I have come to view archetypes as powerful psychological package that includes ideas, images, emotions, and powers. The power of the mother archetype is that of life giving, life affirming, loving, nurturing. Think of Mother Earth.

Think of life without mothers. Wait what? There is not life without mothers! At least not for mammals. This is part of a depopulation agenda to create gender confusion.

The DSM is a work of fiction. Nevertheless, it is interesting to note that homosexuality was removed from the DSM-II in 1973 and Gender Identity Disorder of Childhood (GIDC) and transsexualism were added to the DSM-III in 1980.

The practice of transgendering children is a contemporary form of eugenics as it prevents them from reproducing[32]. In the 1980s, transsexualism was re-named transgenderism and the transgender movement was born. The South Carolina Freedom Caucus sent a FOIA request to the Medical University of South Carolina (MUSC) asking for records of the ages of children given gender transition treatments and the treatments that were given. The ages of the children were 4 to 16. Rather than divulge the information, MUSC shut down the pediatric/adolescent transgender endocrine clinic[33].

Female-to-male transitions have become the overwhelming majority with gender dysphoria occurring shortly after puberty begins. Numerous girls who have detransitioned after realizing that they made a mistake say that peer pressure and social media encouraged them to make the transition quickly.

They report that they felt lonely and friendless. Then they find what seems like an online supportive community that would support them as One young woman has said, "The community was very social justice-y. There was a lot of negativity around being a cis, heterosexual, white girl, and I took those messages really, really personally."[34]

They now realize that they are missing organs and breasts and cannot bear children.

How does this all tie together? Replacing "mother" with "birth parent", forced sterilization, and transgendering children are all weapons in the hands of eugenicists.

The U.S. Department of Education put out a bulletin, Supporting Transgender Youth in School[35], to all schools in June of 2021. In it, they state, "As the Department of Education has reaffirmed, discrimination based on sex—including sexual orientation and gender identity—isn't just wrong, it's prohibited in America's school." Here is one of their recommendations to public schools:

- Adopting policies that respect all students' gender identities— such as the use the name a student goes by, which may be different from their legal name, and pronouns that reflect a student's gender identity—and implementing policies to safeguard students' privacy—such as maintaining the confidentiality of a student's birth name or sex assigned at birth if the student wishes to keep this information private, unless the disclosure is legally required.

Given the highly politicized nature of the transgender movement, the permanence of a transition, the political pressure on social media, the trauma of making an irreversible mistake, and the fact that a young man or woman's brain does not stop developing until the age of 25 — shouldn't schools stay out of this private decision and keep parents informed if this is an issue for a student?

Declaring War on the Human Mind

It may surprise you to learn that NATO and the military-industrial complex have declared war on the human mind[36]. They are calling it "cognitive warfare". Cognitive warfare is now seen as its own domain in modern warfare. Alongside the four military domains defined by their environment (land, maritime, air and space).

In a Fall 2020 report by NATO and Johns Hopkins University[37], they define Cognitive Warfare as:

> *"Cognitive warfare, however, goes a step further than just fighting to control the flow of information. Rather, it is the fight to control or alter the way people react to information. Cognitive warfare seeks to make enemies destroy themselves from the inside out. We define cognitive warfare as the weaponization of public opinion, by an external entity, for the purpose of (1) influencing public and governmental policy and (2) destabilizing public institutions."*

The paper also shares another definition of Cognitive Warfare:

> *Cognitive Warfare is a strategy that focuses on altering how a target population thinks – and through that how it acts."*

> *Cognitive warfare is thus an unconventional form of warfare that uses cyber tools to alter enemy cognitive processes, exploit mental biases or reflexive thinking, and **provoke thought distortions, influence decision-making and hinder actions, with negative effects, both at the individual and collective levels**.*

> *They usually involve a biased presentation of a reality, usually digitally altered, intended to favour one's own interests. New communication tools now offer infinite possibilities, opening the way to new methods and new objectives. This increased complexity should encourage potential victims to develop a*

constant posture of resilience, even if in most cases, victims usually realize they were attacked too late.

— The Cognitive Warfare Concept, Bernard Claverie and François du Cluzel

The goal of cognitive warfare is to destabilize individuals, groups, and governments through "confusion, sowing division, and a means of influence." Could we be a "target population" for cognitive warfare? Yes, indeed we are. The Emergency Banking Relief Act in 1933 amended the Trading with the Enemy Act, to allow the President to use the Trading with the Enemy Act against U.S. Citizens during times of national emergency[38]. The United States has been in a state of national emergency since 1933. U.S. Citizens are viewed as enemies.

The Virtual Attack on the Mind

The one thing that every man and woman has control over is what they pay attention to. As we will see in the following chapter, you create your own reality through desires, imagination, and focused attention.

Remember that Steve Jobs famously would not give his children iPads or smartphones. What most parents don't realize is that young men and women are living parallel lives in the virtual world unsupervised.

Stephanie Boye calls herself the "Porn Mom" and has dedicated her work to awakening parents to the ubiquity and harm of online porn. She tell us that young men have easy and free access to violent porn that uses girls who have been sex trafficked[39]. It is negatively impacting their views of relationships, intimacy, and sex.

If you haven't heard Yuval Noah Harari, a consultant to the World Economic Forum speak, I invite you to search for some of his quotes. Yuval Noah Harari doesn't own a smartphone[40]. He says it is because he wants to protect his time and attention. He only has a landline and nobody has the number. Should we follow suit?

Harari states plainly that the soul doesn't exist and that men and women are hackable animals without free will. How does he want to hack us animals? With technology that was developed by defense departments around the world, but primarily by DARPA in the United States.

The Dangers of EdTech and School Surveillance

The reason that this issue is so pressing now is that, with the advances in technology, especially artificial intelligence and big data, schooling becomes an ever more powerful and dangerous weapon.

> *A massive effort is underway to link centrally organized control of jobs with centrally organized administration of schooling. This would be an American equivalent of the Chinese "Dangan" — linking a personal file begun in kindergarten (recording academic performance, attitudes, behavioral characteristics, medical records, and other personal data) with all work opportunities.*
>
> *— John Taylor Gatto*

Tech entrepreneurs are rushing in to get a piece of the $1.35 trillion schooling pie. They don't understand how learning happens and how humans are driven to learn by personal curiosity, so their solutions are misguided and potentially dangerous.

The end goal is to have everyone working from home so that kids can "learn" from home on the computer with AI as their teacher. If you look at the emerging EdTech companies, they are all focused on "adaptive learning" technologies and AI.

I remember telling my young daughter that it didn't matter how old you were when you learned to read because nobody would know. A friend of mine is a teacher who specializes in gifted education. She told me that gifted students either learn to read early (by age 4) or late (around age 12). With computerized teaching, when you learned to read will be part of your permanent record.

Let's look at BrainCo that came out of Harvard and NASA. BrainCo's Focus Edu solution puts EEG headbands called LUCY on students to track their level of attention. The headband system was first introduced in China because it was determined there would be less pushback from parents. However, when pictures like the one below were circulated on social media in China, the program was suspended.

I showed this picture to my daughter who tried public schooling. She was terrified! She said, "When I was bored in school and daydreaming, I remember thinking, "At least the teacher cannot read my mind."

This technology allows teachers and administrators to force kids to pay attention. It is the most invasive technology I have seen. Why do the creators of Lucy think this is okay?

Max Newton, the scientist who created the LUCY algorithm says: "One thing we're hoping to use this for is to detect users' interest," Newton says. "There's a subjective component people already experience. We want to make it visible and put a number on it so people can learn more about what's going on in their brains."

From the BrainCo website:

> *"BrainCo's Focus EDU is a classroom system that lets the teacher monitor a class's attention level in real time, as an average or as a "heat map" of the classroom, and it generates*

an after-class report on the group as a whole, as well as individual students' attention levels.

An LED light on the front of each student's headband can indicate one of three attention levels, although Newton says the feature is generally turned off during class time. "You don't want to distract students with their friends' headband colors."

The classroom version gives teachers overall student attention reports to see what's getting kids' attention, where they're getting lost, and even whether they're relaxed during breaks. Individual student reports let them see who's having trouble paying attention and when.

Image from BrainCo website[41]

Do you believe that brains are just like computers and that they can be upgraded with technology? If so, then you might think putting LUCY in classrooms and homes so that teachers and parents can control children's' subjective experience of life is okay.

If you understand that a person's subjective experience of life is private and should not be quantified, made public, and tracked, then you will be alarmed by this EEG technology that has been unleashed with a computer algorithm. If you further understand that we live in the experience of our thinking as we will explore later, you will be terrified by this technology.

Perhaps the vision of the men who invented school to completely redesign society is coming to fruition at the feet of generations of schooled and dis-spirited people. I understand that at the core of every human is an unbreakable spirit. We cannot let schooling, technology, and surveillance break our connection to this spirit.

The End of Privacy

AltSchool was created by former Google executive, Max Ventilla, to reinvent school. The startup got $175 million in venture capital to create micro-schools and a new learning management system that replaces teachers with playlists and video surveillance. In 2017, AltSchool closed its micro-schools to focus on developing the platform and selling it to public schools and rebranded itself "Altitude Learning". This effort failed and Altitude gave its technology to Higher Ground Education which now sells it to Montessori schools.

I think Maria Montessori would have a fit if she saw these technology platforms being used in schools with her name on them. My youngest daughter attended a gentle-separation Montessori pre-school, meaning that her older sister and I hung out with her while she was there a few days a week. It was a beautiful environment with a large play yard with water play and gardens. There were no computers or iPads. It's easy to offload learning to a computer algorithm, but it's highly invasive and tracks every thing a young man or woman does, even

One parent whose children attended AltSchool microschools said to Business Insider: "We knew that [Ventilla] was trying to create software that would improve the educational system," a parent of a former AltSchool student said. But, she added, "How can you bring personalized learning to other schools when it's failing miserably at the school you're running?"[42]

Replacing curriculum with curated playlists like those offered by Altitude Learning and the Zuckerberg-backed Summit Learning Platform tracks highly personal data about student's learning activities. More than 100 students from Brooklyn's Secondary School for Journalism walked out of school in 2017, protesting the Summit Learning Platform and saying they weren't learning anything and were concerned about privacy issues.

Below is an excerpt from a letter published in the Washington Post in November 2018 about the Summit platform:

> *Unfortunately, we didn't have a good experience using the program, which requires hours of classroom time sitting in front of computers... Unlike the claims made in your promotional materials, we students find that we are learning very little to nothing. It's severely damaged our education, and that's why we walked out in protest... Another issue that raises flags to us is all our personal information the Summit program collects without our knowledge or consent...Summit collects too much of our personal information and discloses this to 19 other corporations. What gives you this right, and why weren't we asked about this before you and Summit invaded our privacy in this way?*[43]

Invasive Surveillance

In the wake of school shooting tragedies, a school surveillance industry has sprouted up offering to monitor students' every move, including in-school video surveillance and AI behavior assessment, and online activity including personal emails and social media. While the intention may be good, does anybody see how this is a violation of the 4th Amendment of the U.S. Constitution?

A study by Carnegie Mellon University found that, "Beyond complying with federal and state-level requirements, EdTech startups do not prioritize student data protections, as compared to customer acquisition and product development in their first five years." and "Concerns about complying with privacy regulation and guidance do not seem to inhibit innovation at EdTech startups."[44]

Young men and women are constantly under surveillance in the name of safety. Youth are living in the legacy of having no personal rights once they enter the school building. For example Dallas

Independent School District, the 16th largest school district in the country is doing a pilot project using Davista's *Heimdall Student Safety and Support Platform*. From their website[45]:

> *Leveraging existing data within the school, the technology pays attention to students' participation, performance, and behavioral patterns. This process establishes a baseline for each student, derived from their past information, allowing real-time analysis of any deviations from their personal baseline.*

What this means is that they install enough video cameras to track the movement, body language, and facial expressions of every student and match this with the information that the school already has on the students to create a "baseline" of behavior. If a student deviates from the baseline, an alarm will go off to the administrators. They offer "comprehensive tools to monitor the entire student body systematically and promptly". What in the world? How Orwellian is that? Would you like to your every movement and gesture to be recorded and tracked?

More than 60 school districts have spent over $1m on separate monitoring technology to track what their students were saying on public social media accounts.[46] Who is safeguarding their privacy?

Four: How You Were Programmed

Many highly talented, brilliant, creative people think they're not — because the thing they were good at at school wasn't valued, or was actually stigmatized.

— Sir Ken Robinson

The child in a classroom generally finds herself in a situation where she may not move, speak, laugh, sing, eat, drink, read, write, think her own thoughts, or even use the toilet without explicit permission from an authority figure. Family and community are sidelined, their knowledge now seen as inferior to the school curriculum.

— Carol Black

With the tool of free will, anyone can forge a personal purpose. Free will allows infinite numbers of human stories to be written in which a personal you is the main character. The sciences, on the other hand, hard or soft, assume that purpose and free will are hogwash; given enough data, everything will be seen as explainable, predetermined, and predictable.

— John Taylor Gatto

Schooling Makes Us Fearful and Docile

There are two creative forces in the world: love and fear. You can create something from love, seeing that your creation will benefit the world in some way, outside of narrow personal interests. Or you can create something out of fear because you believe that there is something that needs to be controlled, contained, or eradicated.

Schooling started as an idea born of fear, not love. The men who invented modern schooling and created the laws that made attendance at school compulsory wanted to control the "under-class" of people who they feared had the potential to destroy society with their evil ways.

Schooling is an institution that is designed to create ignorant, fearful, obedient, docile people. It has nothing to do with learning or education except that it hides under the banner of education. I challenge you to go into any school board meeting in America. What you will see discussed is funding and test scores. There will be no mention or thought of student learning or well-being.

Schools have become psych labs and our sons and daughters are the subjects of psychological experiments to shape their behavior in ways that are acceptable to the controllers. When our sons and daughters won't passively comply, there are labeled with bogus psychological terms and medicated with toxic drugs that lead to a tenfold increase in Alzheimer's and a 25-year shortening of lifespan.[47]

To force children to go to school where their minds are numbed by boring, irrelevant, and biased curriculum is inhumane. It teaches them to hate learning. Depriving children from being in nature results in their not valuing the earth and life. Pretending that they don't have souls and are not connected to a universal intelligence that many people call God results in anxiety, depression, apathy, suicide, and out-of-control consumerism as people try to buy their way to security.

Adolescence didn't used to exist in America until the 1930s when school administrators noticed that most people were leaving school after their elementary years to go to work. So, they invented middle school and high school to keep kids in school longer. They extended the compulsory schooling laws. School's creep happened slowly and insidiously.

Separating children from society and their community until they are eighteen tells them that they have no true value to society. Thomas Edison, who was taken out of school after his teacher called him "addled" was homeschooled by his mother so that he could reach his full potential. He learned by reading books and avoided math altogether because he disliked it. Edison worked on a night train selling candy and newspapers when he was thirteen. It was natural and expected that young men and women would contribute to society by the time they were twelve.

We Are Wired for Autonomy

A 2010 study by MIT[48] found that un-asked for instruction dampened preschoolers curiosity and drive. The study found: "children restrict their exploration both after direct instruction to themselves and after overhearing direct instruction given to another child; they do not show this constraint after observing direct instruction given to an adult or after observing a non-pedagogical intentional action."

Chilean evolutionary biologist, Humberto Maturana called humans homo sapiens-amans amans or "loving man". Maturana tells us that "love is the only emotion that expands intelligence". He says "...we human beings do not like that somebody else should determine what we think or do; we want to learn, reflect, change... when we feel that we want to change based in our own understanding and choice."[49]

Through his research, Maturana discovered that we are biologically wired for reflective autonomy and freedom of choice.

Humans are designed to be soul-guided. I purposefully use this term "soul-guided" instead of the more common "self-directed" to be clear. We are not designed to direct our lives from our small fear-based ego but rather to be guided by the deeper part of our self that is connected to infinite intelligence.

Learned Helplessness & The Victim Mentality

12+ years of adults telling you that you have no power over your situation while you silently comply leads to learned helplessness. A psychological prison of rewards and punishments forces young men and women to sit still, be quiet, memorize and regurgitate information without any stated or implied purpose other than "it will be on a test". Young men and women begin at an early age to believe that they are victims of a separate, external world (school) that they have no control over.

Before you agree with this view, remember that the school system is a man-made artificial construct that goes against nature. There is nothing natural about schooling. It is more akin to a prison than an educational process. Schooling traumatizes almost every young man and woman that goes through this process of coercion, intimidation, competition, artificial scoring, and shaming.

The Flawed Banking Concept of Education

Paulo Freire wrote a brilliant essay entitled "The Banking Concept of Education". In it, he eloquently demonstrates how education is used by the oppressors to indoctrinate young people to fit into a system of oppression. He shows how schooling is a process of depositing mechanically narrated content that has been stripped of its context. Students receive, file, and store this information as passive collectors of information. He says, "in the last analysis, it is the people themselves who are filed away through the lack of creativity, transformation, and knowledge in this (at best) misguided system."

Freire invites us to redesign education with a problem-solving approach where both the "teacher" and the "student" partner in this endeavor to understand consciousness and how to co-create reality. This is transformational and empowering. It requires us to dissolve the roles of teacher and student and view all participants as channels for fresh insights and wisdom. It also invites us to explore our unlimited capacity for creating reality.

Given the upside-down world that our young men and women are inheriting, don't they deserve an education that will protect their genius and prepare them to solve complex problems?

Schooling Teaches Illiteracy

Most children in public schools who are classified with learning disabilities have reading disabilities.[50] There is a lot of conflicting research on this, but one thing is for certain: whole word instruction produces what looks like dyslexia.

- Only 13.5% of 15-year olds in the U.S. can distinguish between fact and opinion on the PISA reading exam.[51]

- More than 75% of students at two-year colleges and more than 50% of students at four-year colleges score below the proficient level of literacy. They cannot perform complex literacy tasks, such as comparing credit card offers with different interest rates or summarizing the arguments of newspaper editorials.

- 52% of American adults function at the basic or below-basic reading level, meaning that they cannot find places on a map, calculate the cost of office supplies from a catalog or compare viewpoints in two editorials.[52]

Many education reformers and critics claim that whole word instruction was purposefully introduced into schools in the early 1900s to reduce literacy. Whether this is true or not, there have been numerous studies and excellent books that show, without a doubt, that the way in which reading is taught in public schools creates the crisis of illiteracy that we see today.

Louisa Cook Moats found that:

> *Unfortunately, state certification practices, pre-service teacher training, and the social contexts of schools do not adequately prepare reading and writing teachers for the demands of classroom practice. More specifically, neither undergraduate nor graduate training of teachers typically requires the command of language structure necessary to teach reading and spelling well. Consequently, teachers are inadequately prepared to teach emergent literacy, reading, and spelling to beginning readers and those encountering reading failure.[53]*

Patrick Groff, Ed.D tells us that educational malpractice is the root cause of most cases of dyslexia and illiteracy. The Follow Through project in the 1960s and 1970s found that Direct Instruction, which includes Phonics instruction, is the most effective way to teach reading to struggling readers. Yet public schools and teacher training programs across the country continue to use Whole Word instruction.

Since the 1960s we have known that the way teachers are being trained to teach reading is ineffective and yet not much has changed. Don't you wonder why?

Schooling Teaches Us To Hate Math

> *If you only knew the magnificence of the 3, 6 and 9, then you would have a key to the universe. If you want to find the secrets of the universe, think in terms of energy, frequency and vibration.*
>
> — *Nikola Tesla*

We didn't invent numbers, we discovered them. A real math education would encourage young men and women to go out into the world and discover how math works in nature. It would include an exploration of the Numerology (discovered by Pythagorus), Sacred Geometry, and Vortex Math. Chapter 10 goes into more detail.

To understand the abysmal state of math education in America today, I invite you to read A Mathematician's Lament54 by Paul Lockhart. In this excellent essay, Lockhart describes mathematics as an art where the mathematician makes patterns of ideas. He is extremely passionate about mathematics as art and completely opposed to forcing children to do math. Lockhart says,

> "There is surely no more reliable way to kill enthusiasm and interest in a subject than to make it a mandatory part of the school curriculum. Include it as a major component of standardized testing and you virtually guarantee that the education establishment will suck the life out of it."

Rather than the drill, repetition and timed math tests we are all so familiar with, Lockhart shows us that math is "hard creative work" that requires time and contemplation. He goes on to say:

> If teaching is reduced to mere data transmission, if there is no sharing of excitement and wonder, if teachers themselves are passive recipients of information and not creators of new ideas, what hope is there for their students? If adding fractions is to the teacher an arbitrary set of rules, and not the outcome of a creative process and the result of aesthetic choices and desires, then of course it will feel that way to the poor students.

> Teaching is not about information. It's about having an honest intellectual relationship with your students. It requires no method, no tools, and no training. Just the ability to be real. And if you can't be real, then you have no right to inflict yourself upon innocent children.

Lockhart claims that the way mathematics is taught in school is a good way to "permanently disable" young minds.

When my oldest daughter was at dance class, I went to the nearby Starbucks in Barnes & Noble to work. At almost every table was a high school student getting math tutoring. Why do so many struggle with school math?

Irrespective of your thoughts on kids struggling, sweating and crying over their math homework, it's good to know that many famous scientists and inventors struggled with maths the way it is taught in school. Thomas Edison was called "addled" by his school master, Mr. Crawford, and Edison begged not to have to go back to school. He then was taught at home by his mother, but hated maths instruction so avoided it altogether.

> *I can always hire a mathematician, [but] they can't hire me.*
>
> *— Thomas Edison*

Schooling Blocks Access to Our Innate Genius

> *Mediocrity is self inflicted. Genius is self bestowed.*
> *- Walter Russell*

We have been told that genius is rare We are directed to the few geniuses that our society holds up as role models: Mozart, Beethoven, Einstein, Edison. Primarily men. Just happened to be born geniuses. The rest of us? We are average slobs.

As I shared in the introduction, in 1968, NASA commissioned a research study to find out how to identify geniuses to recruit to their agency. Ten years of schooling has the result of blocking access to inner genius in 76% of children. And it was designed that way. If you are connected to your genius, imagination, and understand that you are the creator of your experience, not the victim of it, then you cannot be coerced or controlled.

> *What we have concluded is that non-creative behavior is learned*
>
> *— George Land*

George Land's recommendation is to reconnect with your inner five-year old and rediscover your imagination. Imagination is something you are born with. It is innate. You don't have to "develop" it, you have to remember that you have it and use it.

Negative Conditioning

Our psyches are manipulated, and we are conditioned to be N.I.C.E. by society and schooling.

NEUROTIC - believing your negative thoughts about yourself and the world

INSECURE - believing that you are not enough and not okay

CONTROLLING - trying to control the experiences you have in life so that you feel okay

EGOIC - innocently thinking that you are just a body carrying a brain and need to achieve your goals before you have permission to love yourself

Our thinking is a system of choices that is limited by what we think we know. It is limited by what we believe. And "our" beliefs have all been programmed into us by a dystopian school system.

It's like every person is walking around engaging with a negative thought bubble over their heads rather than engaging in the moment-by-moment experience of life. Or that we all have an iPod implanted in our brains running negative tapes over and over.

What fascinates me, and I hope will capture your attention, is that the conditioned thinking that we all default to was given to us by our parents and schooling.

Programmed to Be Insecure

The root of human suffering is the belief that "I am this small, separate ego and I am not enough". My biggest concern with schooling is that it is emotionally, psychologically, and spiritually abusive. It teaches us that we are not enough. Nobody is good at everything, but schooling forces us to perform in all artificial subject areas according to a made-up timetable. It doesn't matter what our gifts and interests are. We are labeled "good in English" or "good in math" or "good at sports".

We all believe and fear that we are not enough...

- not smart enough

- not beautiful enough

- not skinny enough

- not rich enough

- not loved enough

- not popular enough

You have been trained to compete, fight, cheat, look out for yourself, claw your way to "the top". Research shows that toddlers are naturally cooperative and compassionate (until it is schooled out of them).

We also believe that there is not enough. Not enough to go around:

- not enough money

- not enough love

- not enough friends

- not enough jobs

- not enough appreciation

We take children, put them in a room, separate them from nature and the outdoors, don't allow them to play, bore them with standardized curriculum, force them to sit still, require them to seek permission to go to the bathroom, feed them ideas that are all made up and often incorrect, subjectively grade them, tell them that their personal worth is tied to these grades, and then we ask them to be empathic, compassionate, creative, while excelling in reading, writing, and math.

We never ask children and youth what they are interested in learning, what they enjoy doing, or what their calling or passion is. Most high-school dropouts state their reason for leaving is boredom and knowing that what they are being taught is not relevant to their lives.

In schooling, we break children's connection to their:

- Natural way of learning

- Inner knowing/intuition/common sense

- Cooperative, empathic nature

- Home in nature

- Playfulness

- Love of learning

- Resilience

- Imagination and Creativity

- Awe and wonder

- Soul's calling

- Uniqueness, personal talents and gifts

You have been conditioned to view the world and your self in a specific way. We have been told that the world is cold and competitive, good jobs are scarce, and you need to look out for #1. This is simply not true unless we think it is and make it so.

Programmed to be Consumers

"School is the first impression children get of organized society; like most first impressions, it is the lasting one. Life according to school is dull and stupid, only consumption promises relief: Coke, Big Macs, fashion jeans, that's where real meaning is found, that is the classroom's lesson, however indirectly delivered." — John Taylor Gatto

The insecurity virus is rampant and contagious. Absorbing fear and insecurity, you try to consume and achieve your way to feeling okay about yourself and earn the permission to love yourself.

Institutions and companies feed on this energy to sell us stuff and "solutions" to cure our insecurity and self-doubt. Companies and their armies of psychologists, advertisers, and marketers feed and stoke our inner fears and insecurities to sell us everything from cars, closets, makeup, cheeseburgers, beer, therapy, and self-help techniques.

We now connect more on the advertising platforms of Facebook, Instagram, and Snapchat more than we do in person.

One of the strongest criticisms of western culture is its over-consumption and resulting environmental degradation of the planet. Schooling created this wacky consumer culture by training us to be consumers whose perceived value increases the more we consume.

You've been trained by school to see yourself as both the producer and consumer of your own information. Your value in the job market is based on your accumulation of knowledge – that is only demonstrated by proxy with a piece of paper that proves you did your time. 13 years in school gets you a high school diploma. 6 more years might get you a college degree.

Let's see how schooling props up the economy. Our economy and monetary system is based on never-ending growth. Money is created in our fiat system through debt. When someone takes out a loan, money is created. With no debt, there is no money.

For the economy to continue growing, we need people to work for low wages and to spend their wages by continuously buying and consuming stuff. Why do you buy the latest car, smartphone, fashionable clothes, makeup, home decor, and other stuff? Because you believe that it will make you feel better. Why do you strive to climb the corporate ladder? Because you believe that with a higher position, the prestige and more money will make you feel better about yourself.

You Cannot Learn in an Culture of Fear

Humans are designed to love. Learning cannot happen in an environment of fear. Why? Because with fear comes our natural fight-flight-freeze response. Our body sends extra blood to our muscles so we can flee or fight, depriving the brain of blood temporarily. Apparently, you need to run fast to escape the saber tooth tiger but don't need to analyze it.

To use fear as an instrument of control is inhumane. The institution of school has stoked our inner fires of insecurity and fear to control us, keep our butts in seats at school doing make-work that we usually don't find interesting or relevant. Threats of bad grades, office referrals, in-school suspension, combined with public ridicule and shame, leave students fearful, stressed, and insecure.

Fear is so powerful that it can be passed down to future generations. Epigenetic inheritance is the process through which characteristics are passed from parent to child. In an experiment with mice, it was found that fearful memories are passed from father to baby. Male mice were made to fear the smell of acetophenone, an artificial chemical, through the use of electric shocks. This fear was passed on to their offspring for at least two generations[55].

If our schools can be viewed as a microcosm for society, we see a strange dynamic at play where individuals are encouraged to compete for the highest grades and GPA so that they can be successful and therefore happy in the future. They are pitted against each other in a strange, artificial, academic contest. It's a confusing soup of collectivism and individual competition with the prize being a fuzzy reward in the future.

> *Spiritually contented people are dangerous for a variety of reasons. They don't make reliable servants because they won't jump at every command. They test what is requested against a code of moral principle. Those who are spiritually secure can't easily be driven to sacrifice family relations. Corporate and financial capitalism are hardly possible on any massive scale once a population finds its spiritual center.*
>
> *— John Taylor Gatto*

Five: The Lies We are Taught

Let your credo be this: Let the lie come into the world, let it even triumph. But not through me. The simple step of a courageous individual is not to take part in the lie. One word of truth outweighs the world.

— Aleksandr Solzhenitsyn, The Gulag Archipelago

How Do You Know Something?

This is fundamental. How do you know? There is a whole branch of philosophy that studies this question called epistemology from the Greek "episteme" which can be translated as knowledge or understanding.

I have come to realize that a lot of what I think I "know" has been told to me by an author, speaker, or teacher. How much of what I "know" have I verified independently? It turns out very little. With this realization, I have set the clear intention to educate myself by going to source documents and contemplating them. I am also keen on doing my own scientific experiments to determine what I can verify for myself. And I am comfortable with the unknown. I would rather admit "I don't know" than blindly believe someone else's opinion about something.

Knowledge is a Social Construct

Knowledge is shaped by social conventions, values, and practices and transmitted to younger generations through schooling and the media.

Mordechai Gordon, author of Ten Common Myths in American Education, reminds us of Paolo Freire's insight that knowledge is not a "gift or possession that some individuals have and others lack". He goes on to say, "On the contrary, knowledge is attained when people come together to exchange ideas, articulate their problems from their own perspectives, and construct meanings that make sense to them. It is a process of inquiry and discovery, an active and restless process that men and women use to make sense of themselves, the world, and the relationships between the two."[56]

Men and women are meaning makers. We are designed to explore our environment and the world to figure out how we can best grow and thrive. Two of the best ways to explore the world is through free inquiry and conversation. Both are prohibited in school.

Conversation is the most useful technology that humans have invented for learning. In conversation with self or other, knowledge is expanded. When your mind is at rest, you have an open connection to infinite mind and insights can pop into your consciousness. This is not how modern schooling is designed. Kids are not allowed to speak in school nor are they permitted to freely explore areas of interest or passion.

False Existential Certainty

Every young man and woman is a unique and wonderful expression of the divine with an infinite mind and the power to think good, beautiful thoughts. Everyone writes the story of their life and needs to be able to ask essential questions about it. Real education encourages you to explore the philosophical questions: Where did life come from? What is my purpose? Is there a God?

One reason that schooling is destructive is because, based on Scientism, it pretends to have the answers to these questions. Schooling is designed around false existential certainty and pretends that there is a set body of knowledge that needs to be memorized.

Absent from school is the acknowledgement that there are as many theories of the origin of life and consciousness as there are scientists. Scientists know nothing about 96% of matter in the universe -- dark matter. And most of the scientific theories become obsolete as human consciousness evolves.

How Knowledge Can Be Easily Falsified

The Great Calculus Controversy it is an interesting example of how knowledge can be distorted. We are taught in school that Isaac Newton invented calculus. However, Gottfried Wilhelm Leibniz published his papers two years prior to Newton. When John Maynard Keynes bought Newton's papers in 1936, he discovered them to be full of the study of the occult and alchemy. One paper was titled The Preparation of Mercury for the Philosopher's Stone[57].

There were no mathematical notations and most of his notes were unintelligible. This has led many to conclude that Newton plagiarized Leibnez' work.

The Controllers Write the Textbooks

Parents expect that the knowledge that is being transmitted to their children in school is true, factual, and unbiased. Unfortunately, it is none of these things. You cannot trust the information that is being reproduced by schooling and the media. It is a very skewed version of reality. The history that we are taught in school is mainly fictitious.

The bias in education is based on the belief systems of humanism, scientism, and socialism/communism. School regularly uses articles and news feeds from the mainstream media. My daughter was forced to read an article from NPR on the warming of the oceans for her 9th grade biology class. We tore the article apart together, noticing there was no research included just theories and ambiguous language like "apparently" and "perhaps" that led the reader to the conclusion that men and women are destructive parasites on this planet.

One problem with schooling using primarily textbooks, tests, and highly biased media resources to teach is that it presents a view of reality as if it is the truth. Knowledge is never value-free. All ideas are made-up by men and women and then transferred to others as "the truth".

Mordechai Gordon sums it all up nicely: "Since in almost all cases it is the dominant class that controls the media, advertising companies, book publishers, and other information producers, it is, in effect, able to determine what is considered knowledge." An obvious example is the mainstream media in the United States which is controlled by a handful of corporations and very wealthy individuals.

The vast majority of news in this country is being produced by a few media giants. They ultimately control the narrative. Media corporations depend on advertising revenue for their existence, and the biggest advertisers are pharmaceutical companies. They rarely report news that would offend their advertisers.[58]"

It can be a mind blowing experience when you realize that everything you believed to be true is false. The good news is that once you pull on any of the threads of this Tapestry of Doom, it falls apart. What is then revealed is the mystery, power and beauty of all creation which we are one with.

Schooling Presents a Narrative of Death

There are two main ways to view the Universe: a living, conscious universe or a dying, degenerating universe.

The narrative we are fed in school is that life is a random happening and is slowly marching toward its death through the process of entropy. This is a hyper-materialist, physicalist view of separate bits of matter competing for scarce resources. It is not backed up by true science.

The universe is alive. Earth is alive. Life is a miracle. Life is a dynamic process of creation. Life constantly changes form and never dies.

Dr. Ali Binazir calculated that the odds of you being alive are about 1 in 102,685,000[59]. This is an incredibly small chance. The odds of you being alive are so small, that you have to conclude that you are a miracle. We will explore this more in the next chapter. In the meantime, don't you wonder why this isn't a topic of conversation and debate in schools?

Reclaiming Real Science

We must be free to question hyper-materialism, "the Big Bang", evolution, and every theory that we have been told in school is absolute truth. Let's accept Sheldrake's invitation to reinvent science through reason, evidence, hypothesis, and collective investigation. When you break out of the box that Scientism puts you in, you will find that there are brave scientists making amazing discoveries.

The mantra for Scientism is "believe the science" and "trust the science". If you haven't heard about the reproducibility crisis in science, I bring your attention to it now. Nature magazine did a study with over 1,500 scientists[60] and found that "More than 70% of researchers have tried and failed to reproduce another scientist's experiments, and more than half have failed to reproduce their own experiments." Seriously? They cannot even reproduce the results of their own experiments? And we are constantly being commanded to "follow the science"?

The majority of research and articles in medical journals are financed by pharmaceutical and medical device companies. The result? Biased research leads to ineffective and often harmful treatment modalities[61]. This is especially true in the field of psychology, where the diagnostic and statistical manual (DSM) is a work of fiction used to sell petroleum based pharmaceutical products. I invite you to watch the documentary, Diagnostic and Statistical Manual: Psychiatry's Deadliest Scam[62].

So what is science? I provide the following definition from Sheldon Richman:

> *Real science is a rough-and-tumble process of hypothesizing, public testing, attempted replication, theory formation, dissent and rebuttal, refutation (perhaps), revision (perhaps), and confirmation (perhaps). It's an unending process, as it obviously must be[63].*

The mantra for real science would be "question the science" in order to keep moving scientific inquiry and discoveries forward. Men and women look to the Laws of Nature to figure out how life works in an ongoing process of exploration and discovery.

Do you see the difference between "believe the science" and "question the science"? Science is driven by desire to understand how nature and the Universe operate. Scientism is driven by the desire to get grants to fund research that prove what the grantors want proven. Don't believe me?

In 21st century sciences, exciting discoveries are being made that include the intelligence of water, the intelligence of plants, the electric universe, the position of the sun and moon, the power of imagination, non-local mind, and so much more! We should never be afraid to ask questions, submerge ourselves in nature, explore the Universe, and challenge "the science".

> *Materialism is like an epidemic disease that has to be healed.*
> *And quantum science can be part of the healing.*

> — *Amit Goswami, PhD, The Everything Answer Book*

The Non-Mechanical Universe

Is the universe dead or alive? Why do I pose this question? We are taught that the universe is one big machine that appeared randomly from an explosion. However, explosions result in destruction not creation don't they?

Remember that two of the foundational ideologies of schooling are Religious Humanism and Scientism. When put together, they tell us that we are living in a dead, random universe that was an accident of nature.

We are told that we are meaningless accidents. We are taught that our bodies are made of separate parts and that can be treated with petroleum based pharmaceutical products. We are taught that consciousness is the product of the brain, although this has never been proven and there is no scientific or experiential evidence to support this.

I laughed out loud when I read this in *Beyond Biocentrism* by Robert Lanza who is explaining the Cosmic Egg model of the universe:

In this model, the universe was presented as a kind of self-operating machine. It was composed of stupid stuff, meaning atoms of hydrogen and other elements that had no innate intelligence. Nor did any sort of external intelligence rule. Rather, unseen forces such as gravity and electromagnetism, acting according to random laws of chance, produced everything we observe...

Billions of lifeless years passed with the cosmos set on "automatic" until on at least one planet, and possible others, life began. How this happened remains mysterious to our science. After all, we can take the known proteins, minerals, water, and everything else that an animal body contains and whirl it in a blender until the cows come home and still not have life.

So our standard model of the universe consists of the living and the nonliving. Both are part and parcel of a universe that, cosmology explains, burst out of nothingness 13.8 billion years ago, and the whole shebang keeps getting larger.

This is the story. Everyone has heard it. It's recited to school students throughout the world. And yet everyone can feel how vacuous and unsatisfying this narrative is.

Like the tale of Jonah living happily inside a whale without suffering any physical discomfort, there's something fishy about the universe popping out of nothingness. And not just because in everyday experience we do not observe kittens or lawn furniture magically materializing.

The nature of the universe is a great debate for men and women of all ages. We have been trained to believe everything we are told, even if it's nonsense or makes no sense. Isn't it time for us to go out into the world and explore it for ourselves? When I was pregnant, I was well aware that an intelligence beyond me was growing my daughter within my body. If I tried to use my intellect for the endeavor, I wouldn't know where to begin.

I was taught in school that life is mechanical. The universe is a machine that we can understand by studying its separate, mechanical parts. When I was in 3rd grade, there was an all-school competition to guess the most complicated "machine" in the world. I don't remember what I guessed. The "correct answer" according to my school was the human body.

Perhaps that was understandable in the 1970s but advances in understanding the non-material nature of reality cannot be denied today. If you believe that there is no Creator, then it is impossible for you to understand that you create your own experience through your mind. More about that later.

Schooling Falsifies History for a One World Government

Much of what we call History is the success stories of madmen. — John Holt

What is the real history of the world and the United States of America? You will not learn it in school. The mythologized history that children are fed in school is highly biased towards a utopian future where the mass of people is controlled by a ruling elite. Children learn that collectivism and humanism are good for humanity. Remember, the victors re-write history for their benefit.

The Humanist and Socialist ideologies built into schooling are designed to condition men and women to turn away from nationalism and accept a one world government. The Humanist Manifesto II of 1974[64] makes the following statements:

We deplore the division of humankind on nationalistic grounds. We have reached a turning point in human history where the best option is to transcend the limits of national sovereignty and to move toward the building of a world community in which all sectors of the human family can participate."

The principle around which the United Nations and the International Court of Justice are organized is that the scope of national sovereignty must be curtailed and that nations must be willing to accept, as against what they conceived to be their own self-interest, the democratically arrived at decisions of the world community. Francis Fitzgerald, author of America Revised, invested her time reading the textbooks that are used in school and says this,

> *"The purpose of history teaching in the schools has been essentially to manipulate children's behavior, rather than to teach them how to learn... It's history taught not from the present backwards, but as it were, from the future backwards. From the kind of future that's already determined by the wishes of the teachers.*
>
> *There have been so many studies that show that kids retain almost nothing of what they learn from this. They're bored to death."*

In 1954, a special Congressional Committee investigated the interlocking web of tax-exempt foundations to see what impact their grants were having on the American psyche. The Committee stumbled onto the fact that some of these groups had embarked upon a gigantic project to rewrite American history and incorporate it into new school text books. Norman Dodd, the committee's research director found, in the archives of the Carnegie Endowment for International Peace, the following purpose statement:

> **The only way to maintain control of the population was to obtain control of education in the U.S.** *...The Guggenheim Foundation agreed to award fellowships to historians recommended by the Carnegie Endowment. Gradually, through the 1920's, they assembled a group of twenty promising young academics, and took them to London. There they briefed them on what was expected of them when they became professors of American history. That twenty were the nucleus of what was eventually to become the American Historical Association... The thrust of these books, according to Dodd was that "the future of this country belongs to collectivism and humanism... These educational changes were applied very gradually, so as not to alarm the general American populace.*[65]

It was very sobering to me when I realized that all the history I learned in school or guided my daughters through when educating them was made up non-sense. I am well-schooled and poorly educated. I am in the process of figuring out the true history that has been hidden from us.

Schools Removed Civics Education from the Curriculum

Here are some shocking statistics:

• 43% of Americans don't know there are 3 branches of government in the U.S.[66]
• 66% of Americans don't know what document contains "We hold these truths to be self-evident, that all men are created equal."
• 53% of Americans don't know what the first 10 amendments to the United States Constitution are called.

George Washington said, "A primary object... should be the education of our youth in the science of government. In a republic, what species of knowledge can be equally important? And what duty more pressing... than communicating it to those who are to be the future guardians of the liberties of the country?"

The NEA purposefully replaced the study of the constitution and the science of government with the study of local "social agencies". This is the reason that most people are ignorant of how the government works and cannot even tell you what one of the Bill of Rights are. You cannot demand protection for your rights if you don't know what they are.

From the National Education Association's Commission on the Reorganization of Secondary Education, we get the Cardinal principles of secondary education[67], which changed the study of history and government to "social studies":

*"While all subjects should contribute to good citizenship, the social studies - geography, history, civics, and economics - should have this as their dominant aim. Too frequently, however, does mere information, conventional in value and remote in bearing, make up the content of social studies. **History should so treat the growth of institutions that their present value may be appreciated.** Geography should show the interdependence of men while it shows their common dependence on nature. **Civics should concern itself less with constitutional questions and remote government functions, and should direct attention to social agencies close at hand** and to the informal activities of daily life that regard and seek the common good."*

You cannot participate intelligently in a republic if you don't understand how it works and if you cannot tell fact from fiction when you are reading or watching the news. Most schooled people can do neither.

A 2016 survey from the American Council of Trustees and Alumni (ACTA) found that, "When asked to identify the rights guaranteed by the First Amendment, one-third of Americans could not name a single right; 43% could not even name freedom of speech as one of those rights." [68]

Schooling Hides Evil

John Taylor Gatto shows us that between 1890 and 1920, the children's literature industry became "a creator not a reflector" of values as issues like death, evil, and the future were systematically removed from children's books and replaced by the "individual child free from the web of family and community".

You cannot recognize evil if you aren't aware it exists. Psychopaths have been with us for a long time. The Yupik Eskimos had it figured out. They realized that since you cannot heal a psychopath, you need to push him off the ice when nobody is looking[69]. Psychopathy researchers estimate that 1% of the population are psychopaths. They are usually men and are attracted to positions where they can wield power over others.

Given the havoc that psychopaths wreak on individuals and society, don't we owe it to young men and women to teach them about this disorder and how to recognize pathological people? There is an entire industry dedicated to helping men and women recover from pathological abuse. What if we prevented I it in the first place? You cannot protect yourself from pathological people, psychopaths, and evil if you don't know that they exist.

Society/School vs. Life

As we will discover, science proves that consciousness is fundamental and life is creative and imaginal. Everything that was created by a man or woman was first created in their imagination. Perhaps all life was first imagined by our Creator. The world looks like an idea in the mind of God.

The chart below shows you the way in which our current society contradicts how life really works. You will notices that schooling is very anti-life as are the people who want to control and destroy all life on earth. If this is confusing at first, don't worry. It will make sense soon. Once you see it, you cannot un-see it.

	Belief Systems of Society & School	**How Life Really Works**
Narrative of the World	Separation	Unity
How Life is Organized	Into separate blocks of inert matter. You are alone in a cold, uncaring world	All of life is intelligent energy that cannot be separated. You are like a wave on the ocean of life.
Orientation of Experience	Outside In	Inside Out
Consciousness	Local. Located inside the brain. Inert matter creates consciousness. Ends with death.	Non-local. Consciousness creates matter. Continues after death.
Power of Thought	Thinking is passive and describes a fixed outside reality.	Thinking creates your individual reality. Change your thinking and change your life.
Emotional Intelligence	Circumstances evoke emotional responses and body sensations within us. Learn to manage your emotions and reactions.	Emotions and sensations indicate your level of thinking. They don't have anything to do with your circumstances.
Being Present	Future orientation. Do school today for rewards in the future.	The Power of NOW. The only thing that exists is the present moment. Stay fully open to the beauty of the now.

	Belief Systems of Society & School	How Life Really Works
How Learning Happens (or not)	Information Processing, Give the Right Answer, Testing	Doing, Trial and Error, Play, Conversation
self-Worth	Earned through Performance	Innate
Existential Questions	Adults have figured it all out. Just memorize the answers. Become disenchanted with the world.	Explore, Converse, Decide. Embrace the mystery of life and remain in awe and wonder.
How to Navigate Life	Let your intellect guide you. Use your brain to analyze every situation. Live in your head.	Let your innate wisdom guide you. Your brain is a receiver that is connected to universal intelligence.
The Good Life	Acquisition & Consumption	Creation & Connection

Six: Reawaken Curiosity & Wonder

Whatever education is

it should make a girl unique

not a servant

It should give her courage

to tackle the big challenges, to find principles which will serve as a guide on the road ahead,

Make her strong in the

presence of evil,

Let her love her fate whatever it is,

above everything, it should lead her to discover what really matters:

How to live and how to die.

- John Taylor Gatto, A Free Verse for Kristina

Intelligence vs. Intellect/Thinking

Joseph Chilton Pearce asks us why a child spends 13 years studying a small body of information and then retains only 3-5% of it? We have been conditioned to think of both intellect and intelligence as coming from the evolved human brain.

> *Schooling focus only on the intellect and the acquisition of information. First, intelligence is the capacity to respond for one's own well-being, and so, peripherally, the well-being of one's society or even species. Intellect is a particular form of intelligence, one that abstracts from a broad field of phenomena some narrow part to examine in a linear, logical, inquisitive, exploratory, inventive way. Intellect however, only asks what is possible and is driven to explore accordingly, without any particular concern for appropriateness or well-being. Intelligence, on the other hand, moves for our well-being, or survival and asks, in effect, is what we do appropriate?*
>
> *— Joseph Chilton Pearce[70]*

I love this quote because it shows that we are being asked to respond to life not control it. This is a simple and elegant distinction between intelligence and intellect. We are being guided to respond to life in a way that increases the well-being of all. We are not being asked to judge, plan and control life through our intellect.

If we educate to expand intelligence, then our focus will be on well-being of individuals, society, and the entirety of creation. Let's focus on the intelligence of the heart.

The Intelligence of the Heart

My mind was blown again when I realized the the heart is a sensory organ, not a pump. The idea of the heart as a muscle emerged in the mid-1800s and, while it is generally accepted as true, it has been discovered that the heart is part of the endocrine system.

Rudolph Steiner believed that our view of the heart as a pump was responsible for many social ills. In Steiner's view, if we don't understand how our own body works, how can we interact with the world in a way that promotes well being and supports life?

> *as long as people think the heart is a pump, they will also not be able to relate to outer life in the right way. It is only when people know that the invisible human being is greater than his heart, that it is he who moves the heart, that they will also design their machines to be in accord with human nature.*
>
> *— Rudolph Steiner, From Mammoths to Mediums, 6/06/1923*

The theory that the heart is a pump needs to be examined more thoroughly. We have been taught in school that the heart merely responds to signals given to it by the brain.

The HeartMath Institute points to over 40 years of research that show the heart sends more signals to the brain than the brain sends to the heart. These heart signals affect attention, memory, perception, and problem solving. If you are in a positive emotional state, you will have more cognitive abilities available to you. Fear kills creativity.

> *The heart, an organ weighing about three hundred grams, is supposed to `pump' some eight thousand liters of blood per day at rest and much more during activity, without fatigue. In terms of mechanical work this represents the lifting of approximately 100 pounds one mile high! In terms of capillary flow, the heart is performing an even more prodigious task of `forcing' the blood with a viscosity five times greater than that of water through millions of capillaries with diameters often smaller than the red blood cells themselves! Clearly, such claims go beyond reason and imagination.*
>
> *— The Millennium Report[71]*

What we can say for certain is that the heart is not just part of a separate cardiovascular system. The heart is a sensory organ that listens to the rest of the body. Of the cells in the heart, 60-65% are neural cells. For example, when the thyroid speaks, the heart listens[72].

> The discovery of cardiac natriuretic hormones required a profound revision of the concept of heart function. The heart should no longer be considered only as a pump but rather as a multifunctional and interactive organ that is part of a complex network and active component of the integrated systems of the body...we emphasize the concept that a complete knowledge of the cardiac endocrine function and of its relation with other neurohormonal regulatory systems of the body is crucial to correctly interpret changes in circulating natriuretic hormones, especially the brain natriuretic peptide.[73]

The body is a complex, integrated system. It is not a machine with separate parts. We must stop looking at the human body as a dumb machine carrying around a smart brain. We cannot ignore the intelligence of the heart. As schooling focuses on the brain as the locus of intellect, what human capacity and potential are we ignoring? Why isn't individual wellbeing a goal of school? Are we just creating a herd of conditioned automatons?

Science as Mind Control

Why are children taught that science has figured out all the answers? Wouldn't it result in a more intellectually stimulating environment to tell kids the truth — that science itself is a continually evolving field and we don't know what we don't know?

Wouldn't it be more intellectually stimulating to "question the science" than blindly "trust the science"? Engaging young people in this conversation and debate would be a tremendous educational project. Pretending that science has all of the answers shuts down curiosity and inquiry. Dogmatic assumptions inhibit inquiry and discovery.

Of course, this would create a generation of children who would think critically for themselves, and perhaps this is not what the founders of government schools intended. We need to ask why findings in quantum physics, quantum biology, and consciousness studies are being excluded from K-12 schooling. The discoveries of quantum mechanics began over a century ago. Is it because it doesn't fit with the religion of humanism that excludes the existence of anything non-material?

Perhaps it's because you cannot introduce quantum mechanics without bringing in the debate about the origin of life. There is no scientific evidence of how life first started. The big bang is a theory without scientific proof. Mainstream scientists cannot explain how life forms are organized.

The Mystery of Consciousness

For centuries, scientists assumed that everything can be explained by mechanisms analogous to clockworks. But over the course of the 20th century, we've learned that this common sense assumption is wrong. When the fabric of reality is examined very closely, nothing resembling clockworks can be found. Instead, reality is woven from strange, "holistic" threads that aren't located precisely in space or time. Tug on a dangling loose end from this fabric of reality, and the whole cloth twitches, instantly, throughout all space and time. — Dean Radin

When you start asking questions about the nature of Consciousness, the answers might surprise you. Because we have been trained by materialist dogma it might take some investigation into your own direct experience to begin looking at life through the consciousness-first paradigm that emerged from scientific discoveries in the past century.

Many people believe that their consciousness comes from their brains. However, this is a myth. A powerful myth. Nobody knows where consciousness comes from. Nobody. It is a great mystery. "What is consciousness?" is a question that science has been unable to answer so mainstream scientists ignore the question.

Rupert Sheldrake asks about the Paradox of self-Consciousness: "If I'm conscious of consciousness, if I'm consciously thinking about thinking, I change the state that I'm targeting because my overall mental state is now different."

I regard consciousness as fundamental. I regard matter as derivative from consciousness. We cannot get behind consciousness. Everything that we talk about, everything that we regard as existing, postulates consciousness.

— Max Planck

Quantum mechanics postulates that the origin of life is of a mental nature: universal mind or consciousness. Quantum physics has demonstrated undeniably that the answer we get in scientific inquiry depends on the question being asked and the person who is observing the experiment. The famous double slit experiment[74] shows that human observation changes the outcome of an experiment. Photons act as wave packets when not being observed and as particles when observed.

Consciousness is fundamental, meaning it is pre-existent. It exists beyond time and space.

Today there is a wide measure of agreement, which on the physical side of science approaches almost to unanimity, that the stream of knowledge is heading towards a non-mechanical reality; the universe begins to look more like a great thought than like a great machine. Mind no longer appears as an accidental intruder into the realm of matter; we are beginning to suspect that we ought rather to hail it as a creator and governor of the realm of matter.

— Sir James Jeans, In The Mysterious Universe

Physicalists cannot explain consciousness without a leap of magic. So they tend to just ignore it or give a brief explanation that it is emergent from matter. But they have absolutely no proof of this.

There is no evidence that consciousness is generated by the brain.
None.

> *It is difficult for the matter-of-fact physicist to accept the view that the substratum of everything is of mental character. But no one can deny that mind is the first and most direct thing in our experience, and all else is remote inference.*
>
> *— Eddington, The Nature of the Physical World*

Consciousness remains a mystery to mainstream science, so scientists tend to ignore it. How can you explain the workings of life if you ignore consciousness? Light and consciousness are invisible. They are more fundamental than time, space or matter. So let's explore the nature of light.

> *God is the Universal Soul. God's thinking and imagining creates a body to manifest His Soul. That body is the electric wave universe as a whole. It is God's one idea divided by His thinking and imagining into countless millions of ideas, each having a differently formed body but all manifesting the one by being extensions of each other.*
>
> *— Walter Russell*

Cell Biology

When you look at any high school biology textbook, you will see that every chapter is pretty much the same and every book has a chapter on cell biology. In the 1850s, German physician Rudolf Virchow wrote a book about cellular physiology in which he conjectured that we are made of cells or little compartments. He based this on his dissection of an onion. Many people thought he was crazy. Yet, somehow, this cellular theory of biology and medicine caught on without ever having been proven through observation.

The cellular biology theory teaches us that a cell is a complex unit composed of things like ribosomes, golgi apparatus, and an endoplasmic reticulum. As a recent article by Dr. Tom Cowan shows, "Nothing on a standard cell diagram — with the exception of the nucleus, the mitochondria and a thin cell well — has ever been proven to exist. It's all make-believe."[75]

You wouldn't know that if you read a biology textbook. From a Flexbook Life Science textbook: "As with other scientific theories, many hundreds, if not thousands, of experiments support the cell theory. Since the cell theory was developed, no evidence has ever been identified to contradict it." Really? I disagree. Dark-field microscopy shows only a cell membrane, nucleus, and mitochondria. Don't you wonder why we only see diagrams of the cell structure and not pictures? Where are all the photographs of cell structure?

The Mystery of Light

The world we perceive contains invisible energy fields that we project the light of consciousness onto.

> *Are not gross bodies and light convertible into one another; and may not bodies receive much of their activity from the particles of light which enter into their composition? The changing of bodies into light, and light into bodies, is very conformable to the course of Nature, which seems delighted with transmutations. — Sir Isaac Newtown, Opticks*

Can you have life without light? There are a few rare species that can live at the bottom of the ocean where there is little light, but they are rare. If you put a plant into a dark closet, it will die.

The interesting thing about the world that we see, is that it is fundamentally made of fields of electromagnetic energy. We think that the world is full of light.

There was a famous box experiment by Arthur Zajonc that showed that light is invisible. Bright light is projected into an empty box. Within the box is only pure, bright light. When you look into the box, you see only darkness. "Without an object on which the light can fall, one sees only darkness. Light itself is always invisible. We see only things, only objects, not light."[76]

The lights of nature and of mind entwine within the eye and call forth vision. Yet separately, each light is mysterious and dark. Even the brightest light can escape our sight.

— Arthur Zajonc

There is the light of the sun and the light that emanates from the eye. The two lights are both necessary for sight. Fascinating right? Why aren't we taught this in school?

Physician and photo biologist Alexander Wunsch found that approximately one-third of the energy produced by the body comes from food, the rest is from an unknown sources, which he believes is light. In this model, the body is powered by both food and light.

In 2002, Dr. Solis-Herrerao discovered that humans photosynthesize. He found that the role of glucose was misunderstood. It used to be believed that glucose was the source of energy for the human body. Now it was discovered that the human body transforms light into energy by breaking apart the water molecule. He found that:

melanin's real function in human body is the transformation of the visible and invisible light (photonic energy) into chemical energy throughout the dissociation of the water molecule.

However evidence is overwhelming: glucose is just the source of biomass and water is the real source of energy, a conceptual revolution of biblical proportions.[77]

How cool is that? You can photosynthesize. In this model, the body is a "biological photocell filled with 'living water' that is constantly charged by the sun. Perhaps that is why it is recommended that we spend at least 20 minutes a day in the direct sunlight. It increases our Vitamin D levels and strengthens our immune systems too.

Quantum physicists have described light as the foundation of reality. In *Luminous Life*, Jacob Israel Liberman, tells us, "light and life are the same energy in two different states of existence — form (matter) and formlessness (light). In its formed state, light composes all the matter in the universe. In its formless state, light is a field of pure potentiality."

Light is the messenger of information. Our body emits low frequency light packets, called biophotons[78]. All life emits these biophotons — plants, animals, insects, fungi. Our cells communicate with each other and our environment with light. Gerald Pollack has discovered a fourth phase of water, structured water that is gel-like. Water in your body is mostly in the fourth phase of water. So water is not just a liquid, gas, or solid. Water tranduces sunlight into energy. The sun splits water molecules.

> *We are light Beings (by which photons dissipate into lower orders of frequencies of the entire electromagnetic spectrum having profound regulatory functions). We are nourished by light, and operate by the "drums of light."*
>
> *—Guenter Albbrecht-Buehier, Ph.D.*

We are primarily visual beings and we become aware of what is in our field of vision. The way that most of us believe vision works is a fantasy not supported by science. Let's take a quick detour into exploring how vision works. Each eye contains 126 million photoreceptors. Can you even conceive of 126 million photoreceptors?

The common understanding of our eyes is that they are just clear windows, like camera lenses that "see" what is in the "outside" world. The truth is that the eyes are biological windows that both receive and transmit light.

> *The body is a biological light receptor, the eyes are transparent biological windows designed to receive and emit light, and all physiological functions are light dependent.*

After forty-five years of investigating light and its therapeutic applications, I have concluded that the intelligence of life summons us through light, guiding and illuminating our entire life's journey. Light and life are inseparable.

— Jacob Israel Liberman, Luminous Life

We cannot control our pupils. I thought that they only get larger in dim light and smaller in bright light. Liberman shows that our pupils get larger when we are relaxed and happy, expanding our field of vision and allowing us to receive more information. Our pupils get smaller when we are under stress or feeling down and our field of vision contracts and restricts our awareness.

Liberman encourages us to trust life's guidance system and assures us that we are designed to move through life effortlessly, in the flow of life.

If we trust life, we live in a state of effortless flow and our eyes and aura appear bright because no light is lost. If we do not trust life, however, we think ahead and try hard, losing the light naturally visible in our eyes. The light in our eyes is a reflection of our light content, a gauge of our congruence and coherence with life, which is a reflection of our state of consciousness.

Nature: Intelligent and Cooperative

How can the universe be a dead machine when scientists have found that plants are intelligent? Plant neurobiologist, Stephen Mancuso, author of *The Secret Life of Plants* tells us:

Far from being silent and passive, plants are social and communicative, above ground and beneath, through their roots and fungal networks. They are adept at detecting subtle electromagnetic fields generated by other life forms. They use chemicals and scents to warn each other of danger, deter predators and attract pollinating insects.[79]

I was living in Southern California during a prolonged drought. Many trees were dying from lack of water. An oak tree in my backyard sent its roots looking for water and penetrated the water pipes going to my house. How in the world did the tree sense and find water?

> We all learn in school that evolution advances by pitting each individual against every other in the struggle for survival. As a forester, I learned that trees are competitors that struggle against each other for light, for space. But we are now learning that individuals of a species are actually working together, they are cooperating with one another.

> One thing is that mother trees suckle their children, they feed the young tree just enough sugars produced by its own photosynthesis to keep it from dying. Trees in a forest of the same species are connected by the roots, which grow together like a network. Their root tips have highly sensitive brain-like structures that can distinguish whether the root that it encounters in the soil is its own root, the root of another species, or the roots of its own species. If it encounters its own kind, I don't know if scientists yet know how this happens, but we have measured with radioactive-marked sugar molecules that there is a flow from healthy trees to sick trees so that they will have an equal measure of food and energy available.

> — Peter Wohlleben, author of The Secret Life of Trees[80]

Peter Wohlleben goes on to explain that trees communicate with each other by releasing chemicals into the air to signal that they have been attacked by an insect. Trees have memories and can make decisions.

> Trees make decisions. They can decide things. We can also say that a tree can learn, and it can remember a drought its whole life and act on that memory by being more cautious of its water usage.

Can you really look at a tree as an unintelligent hunk of separate matter after reading this? I have a new respect for all life. And there is so much more that I could have included in this chapter, but it's not a science book. My intention is to show you that schooling takes away our awe and reverence for the mystery of life.

It's time to question the science and figure out what has actually been observed versus what is a speculative theory that has become conveniently popular.

Seven:
Reclaim Your Creative Power

Man creates himself out of his own imagination.

— Neville Goddard, Prayer

When we are not in touch with our intrinsic, creative power, the external power of the state is more than happy to pick up our unconscious agency for us and use it against us for its own ends. If we marginalize our own internal authority, we dream up external totalitarian forces to limit our freedom and create our experience for us, as we see throughout the world today.

— Paul Levy, Wetiko

You are non-material beings inhabiting bodies - you have extremely powerful imaginations and creative power.

— Jon Rappoport

Going Deeper - What are You?

I don't want to prove anything to you, but rather to point you to how you are creating your reality in every moment with your imagination. I invite you to get curious about who you are and the nature of your true self. You can let your imagination unconsciously create what you don't want or you can learn to use your genius and imagination to create the life of your dreams.

Your life is about to get a lot simpler. Most of what you've been told about your self and the world is false. It is time for you to fully appreciate the power of your Mind, Imagination, Intention, and Creativity.

We need to break the cultural trance of suffering which comes from our misidentification of who we are. We do it one soul at a time. I invite you to learn how your beautiful mind really works. It's quite magical!

We have been conditioned to live in the experience of our thinking as if that is reality. When you start observing your thinking, you realize that there is a space in which your thoughts arise. You are that unchangeable space. When you have a thought, ask yourself silently, "Who had this thought?" You will naturally answer "Me". Then, ask yourself, "Who Am I?"

Are You Unaware?

I invite you to the practice of self-inquiry by observing your own awareness. Are you unaware? Sailor Bob Adamson asked me this several years ago. Of course, I am not unaware. "Do you exist?" he asked me. Yes, I exist. "Are you sure?" Absolutely. "Would you rather exist or not exist?" Well, even in my most challenging moments, I would prefer to exist.

The truth is that it is impossible for you to not exist. Honestly, just try for a moment not to exist. You exist whether you like it or not.

Let's explore this Aware Presence that you truly are. Take a moment and focus on an object that is before you. It could be a coffee mug, window, dog. Any object that you see before you. Just focus on it for one minute. Now, tell me - who is focusing on that object? You will say, "I am". Now, focus on any sounds that you hear. What do you hear? Who is doing the hearing? Now, feel your feet on the ground. Are your feet hot or cold? What do you feel? Who is doing the feeling?

Consciousness is the light that emanates from within you and illuminates all experience - thoughts, ideas, feelings, sensations, perceptions. Without consciousness, you would not be aware of anything. You are pure awareness.

The Intelligence of Life

There is an intelligence and energy behind all life that opens roses and grows our fingernails. This is the universal intelligence that turns acorns into oak trees, grew you from a single cell into a whole person, and powers the amazing operations of your body.

Inside of all of us is a boundless, formless, creative energy. Everyone has access to this intelligence. Not just the affluent or lucky. That same intelligence powers each living being. When you look into the eyes of another man or woman, you are seeing that unique, unrepeatable expression of the divine. When you look in the mirror, you are looking at intelligent energy that many people call God expressing as you.

You are alive. You are made of aliveness, an intelligent energy, life itself. You are aware, awake, conscious. Consciousness is what allows you to know and perceive. The light of consciousness shines on all of your experiences - your thoughts, ideas, sensations, emotions, and perceptions.

You are pure, impersonal awareness. Within this space of awareness thoughts arise and disappear. A useful metaphor is seeing yourself as the clear blue sky and your thoughts as clouds that move across the sky. We are conditioned to look at the clouds, not the sky. You are the sky.

Experiencing Your Self as Energy

There is an invisible, all-encompassing energy field of love that surrounds everyone. Therein resides the Higher self or spirit through which the individuals, in varying degrees of consciousness, contact awareness or, unfortunately, may be cut off from it altogether.

— *David Hawkins, MD, PhD*

I invite you to do the following meditation: Lie down on your bed or a comfortable surface. Start sensing your body. Slowly sense every "part'" of your body from your feet to your head, breathing into any tightness that you feel as you scan. Breathe into the tightness and as you breathe out, let it relax. When you have scanned your entire body, take a minute or two to feel your body as a whole. Feel the outer layer of your body, your skin. Then feel the muscles under the skin, and then the bones. Finally, feel the energy that is flowing through your whole body. Stay focused on this energy that is pulsing through your being.

When you deeply experience your body, you cannot deny that you are an energetic being. You experience yourself as a hunk of matter because you have been programmed through language and belief to see yourself as this. You are not a separate hunk of matter, carrying around a brain that generates consciousness.

If you lie down and relax every muscle in your body and relax your mind, you will notice that there is an energy pulsating in every fiber of your being. Frequently when I do this scan, the boundaries of my body melt and I merge with the energy around me.

What I am Not

You cannot experience your true self, because this empty presence generates all experience. You are not an experience, so you cannot experience your true self — pure awareness. A powerful exploration is to explore what you are NOT.

You are Not Your Body

> When you are too busy with material things to have time to listen to that Voice [the Inner Voice of the Spirit] you become chained to the emotions of your body and the demands of material things. You are enslaved by them. The moment you begin to listen to your Inner Voice, that moment you become freed from slavery to the body. The high heavens of God's omnipotent and omniscient universe the becomes your dwelling place.
>
> — Walter Russell

We have been conditioned to believe that we are our bodies. In this belief, when my body dies, I die. Pretty scary stuff. I just disappear into the void?

Is this true? Am I just my body?

I am aware of my fingers typing these words, so I am not my hands. I am aware of my feet standing on the ground, so I am not my feet. I am aware of my whole body. Who is this "I" that is aware of a body? Since I am aware of my body, I cannot be my body. There is an awareness that is aware of the body. (You are that present awareness.)

You cannot be that which you are aware of. You are aware of your body. So you are not the body.

You are Not Your Mind

"I think, therefore I am." Nope. Not even close. I am aware of my thinking. There is an aware presence that is aware of the thoughts that stream through my mind like clouds floating through a blue sky.

We have been programmed to view life through our inner narrator. Let's pretend that your Aware Presence is like a camera lens. We could have the lens wide open so that we perceive everything at once - our surroundings, the sounds, the body sensations, the thoughts coming and going. Or we could focus our attention on a very small part of reality - our thoughts. When we narrow our focus, we tend to become tight and stressed.

Play with this. Since most of our input comes through our vision, relax your eyes and take in as much of the world as possible. Just breathe and take it all in. How do you feel? Now, narrow your vision and focus tightly on one object before you. Stay focused for a minute. How do you feel now?

You are aware of your mind, so you are not your mind. All experience is perceived through the mind. You are not your mind because you are aware of your thoughts. You cannot be that which you are aware of.

You are Not Your Thoughts

Remember the "Banking Concept of Education"? Since you were 4 or 5 years old, you were made to sit still and pay attention and memorize thoughts that a teacher deposited into your brain. You have been programmed with ideas, thoughts, and beliefs - none of which are "yours". Schooling focuses on training brains as if they are muscles. You have not had the opportunity to get to know how your mind really works.

We are held captive by our thoughts, believing that they are all true. We basically are living in our heads. Yet, most thoughts are negative. Most of our thinking is habitual, conditioned programming. Humanity's greatest addiction is to thinking.

We have been taught that all of our thoughts are true. If a really uncomfortable feeling or body sensation arises, I might jump into my head and start analyzing it. This is another way of blocking the emotion and sensation instead of just letting it be. When I let any uncomfortable feeling or sensation just be, it naturally dissolves.

We have been conditioned to trust our minds. Minds are not trustworthy because they have been programmed with layers of false beliefs. You can only experience your conditioned thinking. Billions of dollars have been invested in education and media to control minds.

Once you understand that your mind is a tool of Awareness, you can use it to create a beautiful life. Until you understand that your mind is just a tool, it will be your master and create a life of suffering. Compare your body-mind to your car. You car is a vehicle for your body-mind to travel around. Your body-mind is a vehicle for your Absolute Self to create reality.

The Power of Language

The first way that we were programmed was through a powerful and sophisticated technology called LANGUAGE. Language is not yours. It was programmed into you. Our use of language and how we label "things" determines how we view ourself and the world. Our language has programmed us to live our life in the ongoing narrative of ME and MINE. And to view others as YOU, YOURS, THEY, THEIRS.

I studied linguistics when I was getting a BA in Cultural Anthropology. It is fascinating that some societies have completely different views of time than Western societies. Some groups of people have no past tense, meaning that they don't think of the past the way that we do. When you realize this, you understand that how we view the world depends on how we language the world. Time is a linguistic invention.

The creation of a concept called "the past" is used to control us. The past only exists in your thinking. The only experience that is real is the eternal now.

When you were first born, you viewed everything as oneness. You did not perceive separation between you and your mother. There was no perceived separation between your body and the "outside world".

Sensations and feelings just flowed through. Then you were taught language by people speaking to you and labeling you.

My daughter's first word was "ball". Out of a sea of oneness, she started identifying separate objects and labeling them. Soon, she identified her self as a separate object and took on the label I had given her, "Sage". This happens to all of us. We are programmed to believe that we are separate individuals with a name, personality, strengths, weaknesses, preferences, and a story.

On one level, this is reality. My daughter Sage and I are separate people with unique gifts, talents, and personalities. This identification with a person is necessary to navigate society. We have been given a body-mind to create reality. We are creators who could not create without a body-mind.

That is not the problem. The problem arises when we SOLELY identify as that body-mind. This is an invitation to view your body-mind as your avatar in this game called life. How you play this game of life will depend on your understanding of who you truly are and what is your true nature.

The Absolute Self and the Relative Self

To reach a higher level of being, you must assume a higher concept of yourself.

— Neville Goddard, The Power of Imagination

There is an Absolute Self and a relative self - which one is real? The purpose of our exploration is to realize the Absolute Self and to build a "bridge" to the relative self of mind, personality, ego, body, and time/space.

For the Absolute Self, there is no development or progress. No seeking. No suffering. No attaining. From the perspective of the relative self, there is suffering, seeking and attaining. We need the relative self to do our work, fulfill our calling, realize our purpose here on earth. Therein lies the paradox of our existence.

The Absolute Self is the Aware Presence that you are. It is your essence. It cannot be described. It is not an experience. You cannot attain your Absolute Self because it is pre-existing. It existed before your body was born and will continue after the body expires. It is aware beingness.

You cannot experience your true self because all experiences appear to the true self. You cannot know your true self with your mind, because mind (and all thoughts) arises in your Awareness.

Your Absolute Self can be compared to the empty space in a room. The space is not affected by people coming and going or the furniture in the room. The space is not bothered by anything. You are that space in which all experience arises. You, Aware Presence, is not disturbed by any thought or feeling.

The relative self is your person. This comes from the word "persona" which means "mask". Your person is the mask you wear to navigate society. Caprice is my avatar. Your name/avatar is who you think your are. It is relative because it is an image of you that is constantly changing. Some days I am happy, on top of the world, and feeling good about myself. Other days, I feel like a loser who cannot do anything right. My self-image is constantly changing and this colors how I view the world.

Who is aware of this great show called MY LIFE? What is aware of Caprice? It is the Absolute Self which is Aware Presence. Non-duality points us to the Truth: There is not an object seen and a seer - there is just seeing. There is no thought and a thinker - there is just thinking. Awareness is our real nature. Awareness is the only reality.

We are sold the myth that "enlightenment" is a rare occurrence that can only happen after decades of meditation, deprivation, and effort. The truth is that you are already enlightened.

What is Psychological Suffering?

How does psychological suffering show up? What does it feel like? This is a valuable exploration and contemplation. We want to move beyond a conceptual understanding of suffering and really dissolve it. Once and for all. We are programmed to be victims of an illusory external world. And we suffer.

Who is this Caprice that suffers? Who is Caprice that gets lonely, angry or scared? I am the one who is suffering. This suffering feels real. Who am I? Or better yet, what am I? Caprice is the sum of all of the experiences that have arisen throughout the life of this body-mind. Without my memory, there is no Caprice. I piece together all of these experiences to create the life story of Caprice. This story is not me and it is not an accurate representation of reality, because it is colored by my programming.

I came to understand that I am Aware Presence conceptually, but I still suffered. I witnessed my experience but still I suffered. I still believed that this witnessing Presence was in control and could somehow magically manifest bliss and get rid of all "negative" experiences. I still believed in a controlling entity.

My psychological suffering always occurs around an emotional story of ME and MY LIFE. There is something in my life that I want to change because I think that it is not okay. It could be my past, body image, bank account, a relationship, work. Something that I have judged as not okay and it needs to change.

At the center of my suffering, there is an emotionally charged story about ME and/or MY LIFE. Not just that, but "I" need to change the outcome of MY STORY. Examples: I need more money in my bank account. I need to grow my business. I need to be in a romantic relationship now. These things need to be done and it is all up to me, Caprice, to do it. (Note: this implies that there is a Caprice who is in charge and is responsible for the conditions of my life. We will get to this soon.) Notice that all psychological suffering revolves around a separate person, Caprice.

This all disappeared when I realized that it was my powerful mind that was assigning the qualities of "positive" and "negative" to each experience. This witnessing, judging awareness was not really who I am, but was still generating suffering.

So it was my illusory self generating all of my suffering. Upon seeing this, the game ends. I am the creator of my suffering.

Three States of Awareness

You can experience reality from three states of awareness:

VICTIM: you are a victim of an external reality of fixed, physical things that affect your circumstances. I am a separate person - Caprice. With this identification comes "my story" - my history, memories, personality, strengths, weaknesses, relationships, career, finances, etc. This is usually a highly charged emotional story of ME and MINE. From this vantage point, you try to maximize pleasurable experiences and minimize painful experiences. In this story, there is psychological suffering. In this state of awareness, human suffering is natural.

OBSERVER: you are the observer of your thoughts, beliefs, ideas, emotions, sensations, and perceptions - all human experience. From this perspective, you have some space between you, as the observer, and human suffering, but suffering still persists. I am the observer and I can observe the separate person - Caprice, her life, and the world. With this identification, comes a little bit of relief - a bit of space between ME, THE OBSERVER and the observed experience. And yet there is still a ME and MY EXPERIENCE and suffering.

CREATOR: you are the creator of your experience. By mastering your mind, emotions, and attention, you can harness the power of imagination to create your reality. In this state of awareness, there is the recognition that all is consciousness. As present awareness, I am the creator of all experience. I created the concept/idea/image of Caprice and I create all the experiences associated with Caprice. All experience is created by my mind, flows through my mind, and is composed of my mind. This level of awareness allows us to claim our creative genius.

For me, the shift from victim to observer was relatively easy because I could grasp the idea of a witnessing presence conceptually. So I spent many years bouncing between victim and observer. In some moments, I was thoroughly mesmerized by the story of Caprice and there was no separation between ME and MY EXPERIENCE. Other times, I was able to witness my suffering and striving from a distance as the observer of the show.

I bounced back and forth between these identities and, as I did, the intensity of the suffering changed but suffering persisted. There was still a Caprice that could suffer.

The shift to identifying as Present Awareness was a bigger leap for me, because I was afraid to let go of the concept of Caprice as the actor in the play of life. If there was no Caprice, then what is the meaning of life?

At the end of the day, what we are all seeking is an answer to the question: what is the purpose and meaning of life? If my purpose is not to develop a perfect Caprice, then what is it? What am I left with? If I stop seeking, striving, and achieving, what am I to do with myself? This has been the main preoccupation of my whole life. If I stop looking to the "outside world" to create meaning in my life, where am I to look? If money, status, relationships, and experiences do not provide me with lasting happiness and peace, then where do I look?

The Power of Convictions

*Whatever you **know** you **think** — and what you **think**, you **become**. — Walter Russell*

When you look at the life you have manifested, you see your convictions in action. Convictions are deeply held beliefs that you believe are absolute truth.

On this mental plane of existence, our convictions are very powerful. They have the ability to affect the future - which is a field of probability. If we focus on our current circumstances as the only possibility - then that is what we will experience in our future. If we focus on a new desired circumstance and put all of our energy, emotion, and intention into that possibility, we create a new future.

Your possibilities are determined by your convictions. For example, if you believe that the world is a dangerous, unfriendly place, you will create events and circumstances to make this conviction true. If you believe that the world is a a friendly, abundant, supportive place, you will create the resources, people, and events to make this conviction true.

You are a verb, not a noun. Your life is the activity of aware beingness, the activity of God knowing Creation and evolving Creation.

You are life itself. In this understanding, your body-mind is an agent of consciousness. By consciousness I mean the intelligent energy that permeates all life. I also call this God. It is the intelligent energy that grew you from one cell, that opens roses, and grows grass.

It is through your sense of "I AM" that you connect to the Creator. The creator is working through and as you. You are the hands, feet, eyes, ears, heart and Imagination of Divine Will. The same creative force that created the universe is operating inside of you.

How We Create Reality

Thought creates our world, and then says 'I didn't do it'.

— *David Bohm*

You are an energetic being with an infinite mind and an imagination that creates your reality through your beliefs.

We have all been trained to believe that we live in the experience of what is happening around us. Events and other people make us feel certain ways. For example, if someone is upset, we immediately ask them, "What happened?" This perpetuates the mistaken belief that outside experiences create our internal feeling state.

We live in the experience that is created by our mind. We only experience life through our thinking. By placing our attention on something, we notice it. Our thinking makes the experience a reality to us. If we don't notice it or think about it, we do not experience it.

Notice that all of your thinking is either about the past or the future. We ruminate about the past and our regrets or we fear the future. When we rest in our present awareness, we exist and know. We are just being. You cannot be both present and thinking at the same time.

We don't see life the way it is, we see it the way we think it is. Often our thinking-sensing-feeling happens so quickly that it is invisible to us. We end up trying to control our experiences so that we feel a certain way. If I have negative thinking that produces negative emotions, I will do lots of things to try and numb my feelings if I believe them to be true.

Regardless of what comes into my mind, I know that seated in the middle of all of those thoughts is me - my conscious awareness, my power of discernment, the observer, the witness, my true self...As Divine Beings, we are privileged to create our lives, one thought at a time. If only we awake and remember that we are the dreamer of our dreams, our nightmares, our hopes, and our expectations, we see that the whole creation is ours.

— *Joseph Bailey, Fearproof Your Life*

Your thoughts are the only problems in your life. And you are creating your thoughts. You, the divine creator are imagining problems with your creative genius. It is not the separate illusory, non-existent person (who is imagined to be real) that creates reality.

When you have a positive thought, you are tuning into your creative mind. When you have a negative thought about your self (programmed into you when you were young), you are tapping into the pre-programmed conceptual mind.

If I have negative thinking, start to feel negative emotions, and then realize it's all based on a lie (faulty thinking), I can let it pass and quickly come back to this present moment where there is peace and serenity. We all have freedom of mind -- the ability to choose which thoughts we give life to. And we have free will - how we choose to respond to our thinking and what actions we take. We can use thoughts to make our existence heaven on earth or hell.

Your Mind Creates Your Experience

> *It is not what you want that you attract; you attract what you believe to be true.* — *Neville Goddard, Prayer*

What is an experience? An experience is any thought, idea, belief, story, emotion, sensation, or perception. I've come to view an emotion as a psychological package that includes a story, ideas, sensations, and interpretations all rolled into one tight, little experience.

For example, I used to believe that loneliness was real. Since I believed loneliness was real and true, I experienced loneliness. It came with a story (I shouldn't be alone), and thoughts (this is wrong, I'm a loser), sensations (tightness in chest, overall sense of tension), and interpretations (sadness, grief, apathy). I realized that I could be at a party and still feel lonely. When I decided that loneliness wasn't real, I stopped having the "loneliness experience". This may sound far fetched and impossible, but this has been my direct experience. Now, when I am alone, I enjoy the time spent doing whatever I am doing.

Thoughts, ideas, feelings, and sensations come and go. They are ever changing. You cannot hold onto "positive, happy" thoughts and emotions. If you could, you would. Even your darkest thoughts and emotions will pass.

Maybe I am having uncomfortable thoughts and feelings about something that I don't like and this needs to end. Someone didn't return my phone call. I am feeling bored. I am worried about something. I might try to numb these feelings. I might go work out at the gym, pour a glass of wine, or throw myself into work. Or I might distract myself with thinking.

If you could control your experiences, wouldn't you always have amazingly positive experiences? Wouldn't you know what your next thought is going to be?

Watch your thoughts come and go. Do not believe the endless stream of worries about the future or regrets of the past. It's like you have a toxic iPod playing in your brain all the time. Don't believe the narrator of your life. It is just programmed habitual thoughts.

You cannot control thoughts and they don't need to control you. The reason that you cannot control your experience is because there is no controller to do this. Your idea of your self as a separate being is just that - an idea. There is no Caprice to control the show. There is only aware presence using the body-mind of Caprice as a vehicle for creating the show.

Wait a second, if my mind is creating the show, why can't I control it? Because our minds have been programmed from birth. As we rest in our aware presence, our minds do slow down and we can laugh in the midst of our discomfort, knowing it is all an illusion.

Imagination is our Life Force

You Are a Powerful Creator. You are so powerful. Whatever you believe to be true, will become true in your life. To reconnect with our innate genius, George Land recommends that we rediscover our inner five-year old. He found that divergent thinking uses the imagination to imagine new possibilities. This is the key to staying connected to genius. Convergent thinking in which you are making judgements, evaluating, and making decisions block imagination. Schooling only focuses on convergent thinking, so we forget how to connect to our genius.

Everything appears in our awareness. Everything. We take the formless energy of mind and, through our imagining, turn it into all sorts of forms.

You create your experiences through your beliefs and interpretations. Each of us constructs a self and a world through our beliefs which determine our thinking process. We then choose moment-by-moment how to live in this thought created reality.

When we understand that, we are free. We don't need to take any of our negative thinking about our personal self seriously. After all, your personal self is just an image that you created in your mind. You created the image and the story of your life. With this understanding, you cannot be controlled or manipulated by fear-based authorities, systems, or propaganda.

Negative Thought Demons

Where do negative thoughts come from? Are they really "yours"? When I was creating *Stress Relief 101: Learn to Flow with Life*, an online course to guide you to discover your true self and dissolve limited programming, someone emailed me the website of a man who worked with men and women who had been either diagnosed with schizophrenia or incarcerated for violent crimes. His theory is that the voices these people heard were inserted into their minds by invisible, demonic forces who create negative emotional energy that they feed on.

I put this theory into one of the lessons with a link to the man's website. The day after I added this, I was overcome by negative thinking. It got progressively more intense and loud until it almost led me to have a panic attack. I am not prone to panic attacks. I can only describe it as severe hopelessness, despair, grief, and apathy. I was snapping at my daughters and was difficult to be around. I got to the point where I deeply desired not to exist and felt myself to be a complete failure.

I also sensed that these thoughts were not my own. Suddenly I had an insight. Could it possibly be that these thoughts of self-hatred were being inserted into my mind by invisible demonic entities? Possibly. I got curious. It felt like a possibility.

So, the evening I had this realization, I did three things: I recited the Lord's Prayer and the 23rd Psalm and prayed for intervention from God and Jesus. When I woke in the middle of the night, the attacks felt even stronger. I prayed for divine intervention and instantly felt waves of positive energy pulsating through my body. I fell asleep. That morning, I prayed again and asked for divine intervention to protect me from demonic and negative energies, frequencies and beings. After 12 hours of prayer, meditation, and focused intention, the negative thoughts dissolved, the negative energy evaporated and I felt grounded, centered and calm again.

If I didn't experience this myself, I might not believe it. However, I do think that there are some dark forces that didn't want this course to see the light of day, and especially this lesson.

If we are unaware that such cannibalizing forces exist, we can innocently let them hijack our subconscious like a parasite and make decisions that are contrary to our wellbeing. The good news is that these forces have no power or energy of their own. They have no life force. We give them life when we succumb to fear and misery thinking about our illusory persona.

The Wetiko Mind-Virus

Wetiko is a native American concept that is a "sickness of the spirit" or a "mind-virus" that can attach itself to the unconscious of men and women who are not connected with their inner wisdom, imagination, and divinity. Paul Levy, author of *Wetiko: Healing the Mind-Virus that Plagues Our World*, says:

> *A contagious psycho-spiritual disease of the souls, a parasite of the mind, is currently being acted out en masse on the world stage via a collective psychosis of titanic proportions.*

Wetiko is a non-local field or force which acts under our conscious awareness and causes the inflicted to act against their own best interests. Levy describes wetiko as an inner cancer of the soul.

The important thing for our purposes is to understand that men and women who have lost their connection to their inner light, the light of knowing are most susceptible to this mind-virus epidemic. "People so taken over become programmed like robotic machines in order to spread the infection so as to fulfill the agenda of the darker forces that are driving them."[81]

Wetiko is an archetypal, transpersonal energy that enters through the cracks in your psyche that develop from trauma. Having healed from a pathological relationship, it is easy for me to recognize pathology and evil in the world. I don't turn away or deny it, because I cannot protect myself if I don't know that it exists. References to evil have systematically been removed from children's books. Paul Levy tells us that references to wetiko were also removed from the Bible during several of its edits.

The main way that wetiko enters a psyche is by replacing the image of self as an extension of the divine with self as a limited, powerless, person. Levy tells us that our being has been hijacked by the delusion of personhood. You are a powerful creative being. You are not the limited, powerless, separate person that you have been programmed to believe you are. The solution? Reclaim your creative spark and genius.

Seeing Through the Eyes of God

The eye through which I see God is the same eye through which God sees me; my eye and God's eye are one eye, one seeing, one knowing, one love.

— Meister Eckhart

There are two versions of God that were taught to me as a child: God as a punishing father and God as Santa Claus. By my early teens, I had figured out that God is not some old man on a cloud that waits for judgment day. That is a limited, anthropomorphic image of a vengeful, angry God. It attributes the worst characteristics of men and women onto the Creator. So, I discarded this concept of God. However, it was tempting to pray to a Santa Claus-like God when the circumstances of my life weren't lining up they way that I thought they should. Both of these views are childish and place our power outside of us and discount the creativity of our limitless being.

What if we view God as consciousness? In this understanding, God is the aware beingness that is experiencing life as you. You are the light of consciousness. Consciousness is all that is. You are aware. You exist. All human experience appears in your awareness. If all-that-is can be viewed as an endless ocean, we are all waves on the ocean of life. Connected. One.

It is your quest for the "ultimate human experience" or "enlightenment" that keeps you on the treadmill of personal development. This journey is actually leading you away from your natural state of peace and happiness.

Reclaiming Your Imagination

Your greatest power is your imagination. Do you see why schooling takes 98% of people who are genius and reduces that to 2% of adults? We have been trained to believe there is a world outside of us and we just react to it. We are conditioned to analyze everything with our logical brains. We are taught to believe every thought that pops into our head. The best we can hope to do is notice our reactions and work hard to change them to positive ones. The outside, objective world has the power. We don't. Or so we are told.

This training of generations has led to psychological suffering: an epidemic of anxiety, depression, hostility, fear, and loneliness. It is what we BELIEVE about our experiences that result in our emotions. Two people can have the exact same experience and view it differently, tell different stories about it, and have different emotions.

There is the part of our self that never changes and has always been observing our life from a neutral, impersonal vantage point. It is our consciousness, our awareness. You are not broken. Let go of everything that has happened in your life. Let go of every idea you have about who you are and what you can do. Once we connect with our inner perfection, we stop seeking that which we don't need.

When we realize that we ARE love, we stop looking for love outside of ourselves. We can go into the world and form relationships with people without needing anything from them. We don't need love, approval, or anything else. You are love. You are limitless.

We are one. Unless we are conditioned to believe that we are small, physical beings carrying around brains. You are pure awareness. As Stephen Wingate says, "Be aware and let it be".

Eight:
Learning is Natural

Learning is not the product of teaching. Learning is the product of the activity of learners.

— John Holt

Everyone holds his fortune in his own hands, like a sculptor the raw material he will fashion into a figure. But it's the same with that type of artistic activity as with all others: We are merely born with the capability to do it. The skill to mold the material into what we want must be learned and attentively cultivated.

— Johann Wolfgang Von Goethe

The Invitation

You were designed to learn. Learning is a natural process for you. You have mirror neurons in your brain that allows you to watch people and then learn to walk, talk, and become a self-sufficient agent designing your life from the inside-out. You also have an innate intelligence that supplies you with common sense, insights, ah-ha moments, and premonitions.

Babies learn by watching and imitating older people who are modeling movement and language skills. Most babies learn to sit, crawl, walk and talk without anyone teaching them. Learning to speak is the most difficult cognitive task that humans encounter. And babies without cognitive impairment do it without direct instruction

As we will explore, each individual is unique biologically, neurologically, and spiritually. And every human has an inner voice guiding them to be who they came here to be. When you look at people who have achieved great success in life, most of them attribute their success to following an inner calling or inner knowing.

What is Learning?

Learning is an internal process of getting to know self and your place in the world as you explore your gifts and talents. Learning looks different for each individual. It is an emergent process that is soul-directed, not prescribed or predetermined. Learning happens when a person is able to do something that they weren't able to do before.

The Conceptual Brain & The Creative Mind

You have been taught that you are a body carrying around a brain. Here's how your brain works: you can only get out of it what you put into it. So, garbage in, garbage out. This is the conceptual brain which is the only part of your thought system that schooling acknowledges.

Schooling is based on filling this conceptual brain with information. Schooling focuses on our computer-like brains and intellect. It neglects and disowns our innate intelligence. And we are taught to misuse the gift of thinking. Because of this, we are trained to operate on the habitual thought patterns that get ingrained in our intellectual thought systems early in our lives.

Here's how your Creative Mind works: You create a question you want to answer or a problem you want to solve. You investigate, research, and experiment. Then you leave the question or problem alone and relax as you do another activity. Your mind will present you with a fresh idea that emerges from seemingly nowhere.

How does this happen? Because your creative mind is a part of universal mind - the source of all creativity and creation. You must trust and surrender and be willing to listen to the quiet voice within that guides you gently through life.

The conceptual or analytic brain is extremely valuable. Humans are the only animals who have this gift. But the brain is just a tool of your personal mind. When your personal mind is connected to Universal Mind, you operate from a place of wisdom, not of emotional reactivity.

Joseph Chilton Pearce introduced me to the concept of fields of intelligence. He posits that there are different wave-fields that exists outside of time-space that the brain structure can tap into. In his view, the brain is translating intelligence from frequency realms that are not in the time-space realm. I had the honor of meeting Joe at a weekend long symposium in 2011. He shared amazing insights and experiences that do challenge the collective consensus of reality.

Soul-guided learning acknowledges the wisdom of the inner child in you and your children. Psychologist James Hillman, author of The Soul's Code, introduced us to the acorn theory. Hillman viewed children like acorns. Acorns have everything they need inside to become an oak tree. Children have everything they need inside of themselves to reach their full potential. When they have a desire to do or learn something, it is their soul's inner guidance.

The challenge is that schooling trains us to ignore our inner voice that is telling us school is boring, tedious, abusive, and unnatural.

Mind & Learning

Your Mind is Not a Muscle

This is so important! Your mind is not a muscle that needs to be exercised. Please pause and consider that. Doesn't schooling treat the mind like a muscle?

In response to an article saying that you need to practice math like you do basketball free throws, John Holt explains that your mind is not a muscle[82]. "The mind does not need to be retaught everyday what it knows and understands."

Your Mind is Not an Information Processor

You and your children were not designed to endlessly process and regurgitate information. Computers are machines that were designed to process information. You are not a machine. Your mind is a receiver for infinite intelligence.

By filling the brain with random disconnected information, your brain becomes so busy, you have no space for wisdom to emerge. The problem is that the men who invented schooling in the mid-1800s believed that humans were machines. They denied the existence of a soul, inner life, or consciousness.

Memorizing vs. Understanding

Ayn Rand, in her essay The Comprachicos, makes a valuable distinction between two ways of learning: memorizing and understanding. Rand explains that memorization is achieved by perception and concrete-bound association. In memorizing, students learn discrete bits of information that are associated with each other but not placed into any meaningful or useful context.

"To understand means to focus on the content of a given subject (as against the sensory—visual or auditory—form in which it is communicated), to isolate its essentials, to establish its relationship to the previously known, and to integrate it with the appropriate categories of other subjects. Integration is the essential part of understanding."

— *Ayn Rand*

Understanding is conceptual learning in which you understand abstract concepts and are able to apply them to different areas of your life. To achieve conceptual understanding, you need time to integrate concepts into your reality and make them meaningful.

My mentor, Brent Cameron understood that direct instruction and rote memorization were a small part of the learning process. Used in the context of a meaningful self-chosen project, instruction and memorization can be powerful tools. And they aren't learning.

Economics professor Bryan Caplan, author of *The Case Against Education*, shows in his book that cognitive gains are minimal in college and that most of the knowledge that comes from schooling is "inert", meaning that it can be applied to test questions that mimic the way the information was taught, but people are unable to apply the knowledge to real world situations.

Schooling, with the primary focus on memorization, fills people with "inert knowledge" and conditions people away from using their faculties of reason and logic to come to their own conclusion. They just parrot back answers that they hope are correct.

You might think that this can be corrected by reforming schooling. Schooling was designed this way for a purpose. School is succeeding in achieving its purpose.

How Learning Happens

When you understand how learning happens, schooling will look absurd. Creativity is your life force. Men and women of all ages learn by creating. You cannot teach anyone anything.

Learning Happens When We are Doing

We are wired to learn by doing - whether that is gardening, building, cooking, or reading. We are not wired to learn by passively absorbing and regurgitating information. That method makes us stupid and disinterested in the world.

> *It is a serious mistake to say that, in order to learn, children must first be able to "delay gratification," i.e., must be willing to learn useless and meaningless things on the faint chance that later they may be able to make use of some of them. It is their desire and determination to do real things, not in the future but right now, that gives children the curiosity, energy, determination, and patience to learn all they learn.*
>
> *— John Holt, How Children Learn*

Most Learning Happens Informally

We are learning all the time. From the moment we wake up until we close our eyes at night, we are learning. Perhaps we even learn and integrate our learning in our dreams. Most of what we learn happens informally, not in school.

The science of learning is still in its infancy and most studies are focused on how students behave in the unnatural environment of school. What we do know is that to learn something, it helps to be interested in it, see that it is relevant to your life, and feel that you are safe and secure as you engage with the learning process.

It's time to expand our view of learning to include informal learning, self-directed learning, modeling, mentoring, curiosity, nature connection, internships, and apprenticeships. When you have an expanded view of learning, then the fear over when and how a child learns to read, write or multiply diminishes. Why? Because the 3 Rs are a very small part of education. And they are best learned by doing integrated projects of the child's own choosing.

> *"Any Yanomami father knows that you don't have to force young children to learn, you just give them the tools they need and then let them play...Talk to gifted scientists, writers, artists, entrepreneurs. You will find they learned like a Yanomami child learns, through keen observation, experimentation, immersion, freedom, participation, through real play and real work, through the kind of free activity where the distinction between work and play disappears. Talk to a really good auto mechanic, carpenter, farmer, fiddle player, web designer, film editor, songwriter, photographer, chef, and you will find they learned the same way."*
>
> *— Carol Black[83]*

Your Mind is a Receiver of Wisdom

How do you get your best ideas? Most people say it is when they are driving to work, taking a shower, or walking the dog. They have great ideas, insights, flashes of wisdom when they aren't thinking. When our minds are at rest, fresh ideas come to us. Creativity emerges when we allow our minds to receive wisdom. Another way of putting this is when we are in the flow.

Joseph Chilton Pearce often shared the story of Gordon Gould to ask us what is mind, what is awareness and what is receiving the flash of insight? Why do answers and discoveries come when we are not thinking about an issue?

> *Gordon Gould, awarded the Nobel for his discovery of the laser back in 1957, spoke of that discovery falling into his head in a single flash when he was just loafing around. He spoke of being "stunned, electrified" at the enormity of what he saw in that split-instant, and spent the rest of the weekend*

writing furiously to get down on paper all that this insight implied.

— Joseph Chilton Pearce

This is why it is so important to let your kids play without end goals. Let them daydream. They are engaging their imaginations, which is a straight path to their inner wisdom. You create that which doesn't yet exist in the world by using your imagination and then making your ideas real. As I said in the beginning of the chapter, creativity is your life force.

Education that impairs creativity and imagination is not true education, it is indoctrination.

Free Inquiry of a Playful Mind

When a human is free to inquire into personal interests, amazing learning will happen. This is soul-directed learning. The desire for knowledge comes directly from the soul. You cannot get your child to be interested in something. You can introduce a subject to them and see if they are interested. You can share your interests. One of the most valuable things that you can do is be a person who is curious, playful, and invests time in pursuing your own interests.

The Power of Play

When men and women of all ages are engaged in play without concern for an outcome, amazing learning happens. Test this for yourself. Do you learn best when you are having fun and playing or when you are stressed and focused on doing something "right"?

You can't have real learning with a child unless they are playing. Real playing is how real learning takes place. You can have conditioning, like Pavlov conditioning his dogs; or behavior modifications through other means which we look on

as very serious, and which we generally call learning, but it's
not learning. It's conditioning.

— Joseph Chilton Pearce

The Power of the Individual

During the past 10 years, scientists have made extraordinary discoveries about how the brain works and develops. What is clear is that everyone is wired to learn differently.

You didn't come with operating instructions or a manual. You came with something better -- divine intelligence that will guide you every step of the way, moment by moment. Unless you succumb to your fear-based ego thought system. Unfortunately, because school was invented by men who did not believe that there is a divine or universal intelligence powering all life, schooling disavows this power and trains you to rely on your ego thought system.

The United States was founded on the principle of political equality and the understanding that there are natural laws of individual rights. Why was there such a belief in the power of the individual? Because it is the individual who has imagination, creativity, and reason. Society cannot claim any of these powers. All creativity and inventions come from within an individual.

The Science of Individuality

Whatever crushes individuality is despotism, by whatever
name it may be called, and whether it professes to be
enforcing the will of God or the injunctions of men.

— John Stuart Mill

I'm writing this book as a mother who home educated her two daughters, developed self-directed learning centers, and a global coaching program for homeschooling families. In that time, I've seen that every human is wired differently to learn. My daughters and I are completely different learners. We have unique gifts and strengths, different interests and learn differently.

You cannot individualize education in the standardized school system because it is based on belief systems that try to mold young men and women into obedient workers and deny the creativity and uniqueness of individual souls.

> *The basic answer to the question "Why are you an individual?" is that your body in every detail, including your entire nervous system and your brain (thinking apparatus) is highly distinctive. You are not built like anyone else. You owe some of your individuality to the fact that you have been influenced uniquely by your environment, which is not like anyone else's. But from all that may be known about basic inborn individuality ... it seems clear that the amount of individuality we would possess if we were all born with exactly the same detailed equipment would be puny, indeed, compared with the individuality we actually possess.*
>
> *– Roger Williams*

Science proves that our bodies are extremely individualized from the nerve endings in different parts of our bodies to the neurons in our brains and hearts. Even the information that we get from the outside world through our senses varies for each person.[84]

There is no Average

Todd Rose, author of The End of Average, found that there is no average human, yet we school people as if there are. He debunks our culture of average and shows that human behavior is fluid, not fixed, so we need to design experiences around individuality.

> *If human abilities are jagged, why do so many psychologists, educators, and managers continue to use one-dimensional thinking to evaluate talent? Because most of us have been trained to implicitly prioritize the system over the individual.*
>
> *— Todd Rose*

There are also no fixed career paths because your character traits are independent of how you learn. And as we discussed above, there is no average human body or brain. Once you realize that there is no average, you can relax knowing that there is no standard to compare your child to.

Your Inner Calling

If you carefully observe newborns, you will notice a natural wisdom and peace when they are not hungry, tired or wet. When my oldest daughter was two days old, I gently laid her down to sleep. Her eyes flew open and she looked deep into my soul. I saw depths of wisdom and love that I didn't expect. At that moment, I knew that she was a soul sent here to guide and teach me.

It is assumed that human suffering is just a normal part of the human experience. What if this isn't normal? What if it is a result of a schooling system and society that was designed from fear?

It might be tricky to see how schooling conditions humans to use their thinking against themselves. It is generally assumed that school is a positive and necessary institution. Any suffering is attributed to individual dysfunction. If this is true, why is human suffering at epidemic levels? Young people are inherently resilient and creative and are doing their best to survive an institution that systematically denies their inner lives and impedes their creativity, imagination, and innate wisdom.

You are not a mechanical widget that came here without a purpose. Remember, the odds of you being alive are so small, that you have to conclude that you are a miracle. Your soul speaks to you through desire. When you desire to learn or do something, pay attention to it. Your inner wisdom is speaking to you.

> *"You possess a kind of inner force that seeks to guide you toward your Life's Task— what you are meant to accomplish in the time that you have to live. In childhood this force was clear to you. It directed you toward activities and subjects that fit your natural inclinations, that sparked a curiosity that was*

deep and primal. In the intervening years, the force tends to fade in and out as you listen more to parents and peers, to the daily anxieties that wear away at you. This can be the source of your unhappiness— your lack of connection to who you are and what makes you unique. The first move toward mastery is always inward— learning who you really are and reconnecting with that innate force. Knowing it with clarity, you will find your way to the proper career path and everything else will fall into place. It is never too late to start this process."

— Robert Greene, Master

Schooling trains you to mute this desire and inner wisdom. It is time to honor and cultivate it. At first, it may seem like a quiet whisper that is a stranger to you. As you cultivate deep listening, you will learn to trust your inner calling. Remember: if you are lost, confused, or uncertain, then quit your mind and listen. When you are listening, you aren't thinking. Thinking and analyzing is not the path to clarity.

Planet Earth is most definitely not the center of your personal life. It's merely a background which floats in and out of conscious thought. The truth is that both psychologically and spiritually you are the center of the solar system and the universe. Don't be modest or try to hide the fact. The minute you deny what I just said, you're in full flight from the responsibility this personal centrality entails: to make things better for the rest of us who are on the periphery of your consciousness.

— John Taylor Gatto

The net result of schooling/social engineering is generations of people who are insecure, fearful, and confused. They feel alone and afraid in a cold, uncaring world. They have lost touch with their inner guidance system and are propelled along the conventional path of achievement and success.

At a time when we need human ingenuity, we continue to march young people through a system built for compliance, not wisdom. Welcome to the joyful world of deprogramming. Let's get started!

You cannot connect with your true self through your intellect or by seeking with thinking. You must go deeper and go within. Within is not a physical place, it is the place that existed before form.

Your mind is the source of your intelligence. Your brain is a tool of the mind. Your personal mind is connected to a universal mind that guides you lovingly through life. Your personal intellect is a tool that can be used by your intelligence, but it is only a tool.

Learning vs. Social Engineering

Achievement

Truth: You cannot achieve your way to happiness or peace of mind.

Social Engineering: Academic achievement is the game of schooling. Whoever processes the most information wins. Children are told explicitly and implicitly that their value and self-worth is dependent upon their achievement in a narrow band of academic activities. The worth/value of students is measured by grades and obedience. Children who are good with symbols and rote memorization and learn in an auditory-sequential way win the game of schooling.

Comparison

Truth: You are a unique expression of the divine. You are unique, but not special. Comparing yourself to anyone will cause suffering.

Social Engineering: Students are continually compared and sorted by teachers and administrators. Parents compare the achievements of their children in school to other kids. "My kid is an honor roll student" bumper stickers are everywhere. Grades, GPA, honor roll, and college scholarships are all used to psychologically manipulate children to perform and achieve.

Competition

Truth: Our ground of being is infinite mind. We are all connected, so there is no need to compete. Do your best and let go of the outcome. You are not in control.

Social Engineering: Students are conditioned to compete for scarce resources (grades, praise, honor roll, etc.)

Fear

Truth: You feel fear when you experience your own fearful thinking. Fear is good when a fight/flight/freeze response could save your life from imminent danger, otherwise it's just a lie your thinking is producing.

Social Engineering: Uses fear as a weapon of control. Students are threatened with disciplinary action for breaking the rules: coming to school with an uncharged computer, not wearing the proper uniform, talking in class, not doing homework, not following random rules, going to the bathroom without a hall pass.

Shame

Truth: You are unbreakable and at your core you are pure love and consciousness.

Social Engineering: You are bad if you don't do your schoolwork, do poorly on a test, or break the rules.

Sacrificing the Joy of Presence for Future Rewards

Truth: There is no past or future. The only thing that exists is the eternal now.

Social Engineering: Work hard now for promised rewards in the future.

The Inner Voice

Truth: You will be guided every moment by universal Mind that comes to you as a loving, calm, quiet voice.

Social Engineering: Sit still, be quiet, and listen to the teacher. Ignore your body if it wants to move.

Consciousness

Truth: You are conscious and aware. This consciousness allows you to experience your thought-created reality. Your personal mind is connected to infinite mind.

Social Engineering: Consciousness is the by-product of an advanced brain. It exists locally within your brain and will disappear when you die. There is no inner life of the individual.

Imagination

Truth: Your beliefs shape your reality. Imagination is a creative power. You can imagine a world based on desires not past programming.

Social Engineering: Thinking is an analytic skill that you need to develop by processing information. Thinking is passive and describes an outside reality. Students are taught to navigate life with their intellect, analyzing situations to make decisions. They end up living in their heads.

Feelings

Truth: Feelings are your inner GPS system that tells you if you are thinking productive, helpful thoughts, or negative, destructive thoughts.

Social Engineering: Doesn't acknowledge the inner life of children (or adults).

Nine: De-School Your self

Nothing is more pathetic than people who run around in circles, "delving into the things that lie beneath" and conducting investigations into the souls of the people around them, never realizing that all you have to do is to be attentive to the power inside you and worship it sincerely.

— *Marcus Aurelius*

10 Reasons to Deschool Your Family

1. Reconnect with awe and wonder as you explore how life, the Laws of Nature, and the universe really operate.
2. Protect every individual's genius, happiness, peace, creativity, resilience, and connection with the Creator.
3. Strengthen your imagination, intuition and inner voice.
4. Focus on personal strengths (not weaknesses).
5. Learn how each person is uniquely wired to learn.
6. Remove all limits to learning and creating.
7. Experience thriving in life, not just surviving school.
8. Create something awesome (instead of just processing information and obeying random authorities).
9. Explore gazillions of free and low-cost learning resources and experiences - that are fun, engaging, and relevant.
10. Learning is easier and more fun than schooling

The Right to Educate Yourself

We hold these truths to be self-evident, that all men are created equal, that they are endowed by their Creator with certain unalienable Rights, that among these are Life, Liberty, and the pursuit of Happiness.

— The Declaration of Independence

Forced government schooling cannot exist in a just society. People with a socialist belief system will claim that schooling levels the socio-economic playing field. It certainly does not. Research shows that schooling perpetuates economic inequalities.

The right to educate yourself is a natural human right, not one given to you by any government. Notice I didn't say the right to schooling is a natural human right. Schooling is an institution that was invented by men. Education is required by nature for each individual to learn how to adapt to their unique environment.

With the explosion of learning opportunities and information available on the Internet, learning can happen anywhere and anytime. Online courses and schools, free open courses from prestigious universities, games-based learning, Maker Clubs, 3D printing, and coding schools are low-cost options that can be made available to everyone for a lot less than the $13,000 we spend per student per year for schooling.

People survive in this complex society by using their minds and reason so that they can get their needs met. After the age of 18, it is up to the individual to take action to get needs met. Because we are a species that lives in complex social groups, unless you are living on a self-sufficient farm off the grid, you need to learn to live in society among your fellow humans.

Your ability to successfully navigate this complex society and pursue happiness depends upon your ability to use your mind, connect with your inner wisdom, think critically, and practice self-care. By educating yourself, you get to know yourself and the world, learn how to think, and gradually become responsible for your own life.

Today, if you are not legally homeschooling your children or have them in a public or private school, the government will take your children from you. So, do you really think that you are free?

The Purpose of Soul-Directed Learning

"The goal of real education is to bring us to a place where we take full responsibility for our own lives."

— John Taylor Gatto

We come into this world as free beings connected to our innate wisdom and wellbeing. We let our thoughts and emotions pass through without hooking us. We have free will and choose where to focus our attention. We are free from fear and do not judge. We are naturally curious, resilient, altruistic, cooperative. We thrive in nature and through play. Energy flows through our body, encouraging us to move.

We are designed to learn so that we grow into self-sufficient beings who self-direct our learning and lives. Learning is a natural, internal process of awakening to self that best happens as the free inquiry of a relaxed, peaceful, playful mind. We need to trust that humans are designed to learn, and desire is the calling of their soul to learn something. It may be dance, painting, building, writing, or molecular biology. The point is that it is their choosing.

Why do we educate our young? Young people discover who they are and how they can function successfully in the world by participating in it. Learning is not an object or thing that can be tracked and measured. It cannot be forced.

Indigenous people understood this, so children learned in the community, observing adults, modeling their behavior, and adapting to their environment. Children in industrialized countries are forced to adapt to the artificial, pathological environment of schooling away from the rest of society. As they grow, they awaken to an artificial self. They are taught to survive school and not thrive in life.

We don't teach humans how to learn. The mind is not a muscle that needs to be exercised. And it is not a machine that needs to be filled with information. Filling a brain with random information and training us to live in our heads, mesmerized by our thinking blocks our ability to receive wisdom.

Many people believe that formal education within a school institution where a teacher is leading the educational activity is the only worthwhile endeavor. Most parents have been conditioned to think that they are incapable of educating their children.

Often, I encounter mothers who look at me and say how brave I am for home educating my kids. Or they ask me how I can stand being with my kids every day. What this points to is a widespread misunderstanding of learning and education.

Soul guided education produces secure, independent, literate people who can think for themselves and have self-agency.

Education done well is mastery of self, evolution of consciousness, exploration of gifts and talents, and complete well-being (mental, emotional, physical, psychological, spiritual, and financial). Notice that this list doesn't include information processing and mastery of subject matter.

Education can guide you to understand how your mind and imagination work, how you create your own reality, what your innate skills and talents are and how you want to contribute your gifts to society. Education is not a group activity; it is an individual process that can be greatly enhanced by belonging to an educational community.

Begin by De-Schooling Yourself

I had to ignore my inner knowing to survive school. Regaining a connection to my soul and inner purpose has been an interesting journey.

Fortunately, humans are designed to thrive. This book isn't just about the mechanics of successful education outside of schooling, it is about the joy of learning and living. Our design is beautiful and magnificent. Not even schooling can break our spirits.

If you were schooled into thinking that your self-worth is attached to performance, achievement, grades, teacher approval, then it's time to wake up and re-jigger your estimation of yourself. There is no correlation between success in school and success in life. The average GPA of millionaires is 2.9.

If you continue to believe that your self-worth is connected to your stuff (house, car, job title, clothes, etc.), your credit score, your performance review, or your number of social media friends, then it's time to wake up and start living your own life.

If you were schooled to think that you are a passive participant in your own life, it is time for you to begin to create the life that you want to live. And stop schooling your kids. The "I suffered through it, they will too" argument is just a symptom of the Prisoner's Dilemma

The False Beliefs You Were Taught by Schooling

Myth #1: You are alone in a cold, uncaring world.

The schooling paradigm is built on a story of a dead, random universe. We are sold the false theories of the Big Bang, evolution to make use feel that our lives are an accident, we are not connected to the Creator, so we might as well pursue pleasures without any moral compass.

As long as we believe that we are separate blocks of physical matter that need to compete for scarce resources (grades, honor roll, GPA, jobs, money, status, stuff) then we will continue our fear-based journey of trying to control all of our experiences so that we feel okay and safe.

It's not your fault. You have been conditioned to view the world in this way and are doing the best you can inside of this false worldview.

Result: We are stressed, anxious, fearful, depressed, apathetic, and lonely.

Myth #2: Imagination is not a creative force.

We are conditioned to use reactive thinking, not creative thinking. Things happen and we react, then we think and say, "Well of course I'm upset, you would be upset too if you had the same experience." Life becomes a continuous reaction to outside stimuli. You are sad or happy and decide if life has meaning or is meaningless using what happens to you day to day as evidence.

We are the creators of our own experiences. Imagination is the most powerful force in the world. We create our life stories through our beliefs and habitual thoughts. When we realize that we are living in the thought created reality, we have the opportunity to change our relationship to our thinking. We are free to write an awesome life story and enjoy every moment. We harness the divine gift of imagination to transform our lives.

Result: We live in our heads, constantly processing information, hoping for peace and happiness at the end of a thought storm. We are deprived of the joy of being alive.

Myth #3: Your intellect defines who you are

Our brains are fabulous tools of our greater mind that we can use to process and analyze information. A mind is a great thing to use to change a tire or cook a meal. Schooling disconnects us from our imagination and creative thinking that is always available to us. We are trained like flesh-covered robots to process information and obey. Your self-worth is measured by how much information you process. Men and women are not designed for information processing.

Result: The artificial measuring stick of schooling makes us all feel like impostors.

Myth #4: Life is to be conquered, not to be held sacred

When kids are allowed free time in nature, they stay enchanted with the natural world. If they are able to engage in fresh scientific discovery and philosophical debates, they will love learning. Schooling pretends that adults have figured it all out and a kid's job is to memorize the facts of life. Did you know we are in the middle of a new scientific revolution that will turn everything you think on its head? This makes standards, standardized curriculum, and testing an incredible waste of time and resources.

Result: A boring, rigid schooling system blocks free play, nature immersion, inquiry, philosophy, and conversation. We lose the awe and wonder of being alive and creative.

Myth #5: You need to obey

You've been psychologically manipulated to reflexively obey outside authorities no matter what cost. School's laser focus on standardized information processing requires a culture of coercion. Teachers are forced to march kids through standardized, mind-numbing, often inaccurate curriculum. Schooling takes away our free will and the power of choice. We are not allowed to choose what we think, what we learn, how we learn it, or who our teachers and mentors are.

Result: We're busy chasing a false promise of future happiness and obeying outside authorities while our lives slip by.

What are Your Own Schooling Wounds?

To joyfully home educate your children, you need to recognize that you got some wounds in your schooling experience. Kirsten Olson wrote an excellent book called Wounded By School. She set out to interview successful people and find out how their school experience contributed to their success. She discovered that everyone had deep wounds from school and succeeded in spite of their schooling. Peter Gray offers an excellent summary of Wounded by School in his Psychology Today Blog

I co-created a global coaching program for homeschooling families and quickly learned that we all believe our school experience was somehow lacking. We then try to make up for what we didn't get by giving whatever we were missing to our children. It's helpful to see if we are trying to meet our old, unmet needs or the current needs of our individual children. You will learn this through trial and error. Give yourself permission to be flexible so that you can change course quickly when something is not working. As we will explore in Ages and Stages, your child's needs will change over time.

I had no freedom in school, so I gave my daughters lots of freedom. My oldest daughter enjoys structure and someone to choose her projects for her, so I learned to create enough structure and guidance for her so that she feels safe. My youngest daughter is highly self-directed and wants ultimate freedom. So, even in your home, you will adjust the environment to meet individual needs.

One mom that I coached had attended a free school in the desert of New Mexico. She felt that her school experience was too loose and that she didn't get the academic rigor that she wanted, so she initially chose a highly regimented, academically focused program for her kids. She didn't realize that she was trying to meet her own needs not those of her children.

By recognizing your own wounds and unmet needs, you can own them for yourself and not project them onto your kids. My wounds in school are all of the psychological variety. See if any of these are familiar to you.

- I often feel insecure. After years of competing for grades and high GPAs, I have been trained to compare myself to other people. I know that this is a losing game, but it seems to have been drilled into me. There will always be someone that looks more successful or better than me, so I have to remind myself that I am using my thinking against myself. I feel insecure because I am having insecure thinking and this was encouraged in school.

- I'm afraid to be late. The tyranny of the bells in school and fear of missing the school bus still activate fear in my body.

- I hate making a mistake. I believe that it shows I am somehow worthless. I see how school only rewards the right answer and an A is much better than a C, even if you only learned something long enough to do well on a test. I'm just giving myself permission to make mistakes because I know that is the only way to learn something new.

- I fear the unknown. I often procrastinate when starting something new because I don't already know how to do it. I see how schooling discouraged risk taking.

Schooling is an unnatural way of learning that forces kids to learn the same things and the same time irrespective of interest or ability. Because schooling is so excruciatingly boring and irrelevant, teachers resort to fear and shame to coerce kids to jump through antiquated academic hoops.

We have been conditioned to value ourselves by arbitrary grades created by outside authorities. If we got bad grades, we think we're stupid. If we got good grades, we will often stay on the performance and achievement treadmill for life. It doesn't matter that only 5% of people learn in the auditory-sequential-symbolic way that school teaches information. Most of us secretly harbor the belief and fear that we are not okay. We were taught this in school.

Our culture is increasingly fear-based. Negative thought patterns about self and the world are reproduced and reinforced in school.

To live a creative life, we must lose our fear of being wrong.

– Joseph Chilton Pearce

When deciding about their children's education, most parents make a decision based in fear. They are afraid of making a mistake and their children will be left behind. Fear is always an indication that you are thinking fearful thoughts, but it has nothing to do with the outside world unless you are encountering a bear or a snake.

Learn to trust the natural learning process. Your child has innate wisdom that is always guiding her just like you have innate wisdom guiding you. I talk about self-directed education frequently, and here I am going to switch gears and call it soul-directed learning.

I lost count of the times another mother has told me how brave I am to homeschool my children. And yet, year and year as August approaches, I hear them hope that their child gets a good teacher and laments the bad teachers from last year or the kids that bullied their child. To me, they are playing Russian Roulette with their child's education. I have never had to hope that my kids will get a good teacher or not get bullied.

And I don't put pressure on myself to be a perfect teacher, because I am more of a guide on the side. I encourage their interests, I strew books and materials around the house, and most importantly, I operate from love not fear.

As I will show in the following chapters, there are no "basics" to master, there is no critical information to memorize, there is no way that your child will fall behind. Learning is not a race. There are no winners. There are young people who are enchanted with the world, love to play and are naturally wired to learn and grow.

Brent Cameron, co-founder of selfDesign, often likened schooling to gluing wings to a caterpillar. It just doesn't work. In his famous TED talk[85], Sir Ken Robinson shows how schools kill creativity and points out that our school system is designed to produce college professors.

Ten: Protecting Young Minds

*All I am saying in this book can be summed up in two words—
Trust Children. Nothing could be more simple - or more
difficult. Difficult, because to trust children we must trust
ourselves - and most of us were taught as children that we
could not be trusted.*

— John Holt, How Children Learn

*Giving our children control of their own education is certainly
a risky business. All guarantees that they are keeping pace
with their peers are abandoned and replaced with a simple
trust that they will explore life of their own initiative.*

— Brent Cameron

Let's Evolve Human Consciousness

We have a fundamental responsibility to awaken and educate young people in a way that evolves human consciousness. To change the trajectory of the human project, we need a new narrative of who we are, how learning happens, and what it takes to create a just and free society. To do this, we have to challenge the current paradigm that leads to separation, fear, and the quest to control life.

The fatal flaw of the schooling paradigm is that it was designed from FEAR. When you look at direct quotes from the men who invented and championed government schooling in the mid-1800s and early 1900s, their fear and arrogance is visible. Children are treated like deficient machines that need to be molded into productive citizens that can be controlled. In this game, the student who is the most obedient and processes the most information wins.

Children are being conditioned to survive school rather than thrive in life. Schooling falsely claims that learning is a mechanical process best undertaken in neo-Darwinistic competitive individualism same-age classrooms following standardized curriculum. Hopefully, you can see that this is a false paradigm and it's time to evolve beyond it.

When we educate to preserve innate wholeness, wisdom and wellbeing, young people will unleash their unlimited capacity to innovate. They can evolve the world and society in a positive direction through their insights.

What Do You Believe?

If you believe that...

- There is no creative force, higher power or God in the universe.

- Science and technology are the supreme powers that will solve all earthly problems.

- Children enter the world as completely blank slates, with no soul or calling.

- They will become bad and useless unless trained otherwise.

- Children must be forced to learn because they are lazy.

- We need to be controlled by a powerful, centralized state that is led by self-chosen elites, otherwise it will be chaos.

- An under-educated class of workers-consumers is an essential part of the design.

Then forced government schooling is your solution.

If you believe (like me) that...

- Life is a wonderful, awe-inspiring mystery and chances are good that there is a universal intelligence, consciousness, or God that exists.

- Humans are part of nature, not outside of it or above it.

- The use of technology is best moderated by wisdom.

- Humans are naturally curious and designed to learn.

- Children are inherently resilient, cooperative, and empathic.

- Each child is unique with gifts, talents, a calling and a purpose.

- Human creativity, ingenuity, and entrepreneurship are positive forces that can be encouraged and expanded.

- People have an innate drive to create, not consume.

Then begin your soul guided learning journey.

Humans are born:	Until they are conditioned to become:
INNOCENT	UNETHICAL
WISE	UNAWARE
CURIOUS	APATHETIC
SECURE	INSECURE
CREATIVE	CONSUMERS
COOPERATIVE	COMPETITIVE
ALTRUISTIC	SELFISH

What is Your Why?

It's okay if you aren't clear at this moment. As with anything in life, once you get really clear about your why, it becomes easier to stay the course when you hit bumps in the road. And you will have glorious days and ones where you wish you would have stayed in bed.

I believe that the goal of education is empowered, awakened individuals who use their minds, creativity, and energy to co-create a free and fair society and healthy biosphere. I invite you to create a why for your family that is separate from the agenda of schooling.

I read an excellent book by Jon and Myra Kabat-Zinn soon after my first daughter was born called everyday blessings: the inner work of mindful parenting. I highly recommend it! For me, it reframed my mothering journey as a spiritual one. This helped on the day that my youngest daughter, not yet 2 at the time, bit me three times. Ouch!

My why for home educating my daughters has changed over the years. First, it was to protect them from the sheer boredom of schooling and give them time and space to discover themselves. Later, I realized that I wanted them to be able to think for themselves and didn't want them to be institutionalized.

I led a workshop at the California Homeschool Association conference in 2009 entitled Trust. It was focused on helping parents learn to trust their kids and the natural learning process. I started the workshop by asking parents what they truly wanted for their kids. The consensus was they all wanted their kids to be happy. Nobody mentioned good at math, writing, or social studies. So, I'm guessing that you are home educating or considering home educating your kids because you love them and want them to be happy. That's enough of a why for anyone.

Getting Started - Make Learning and Creating a Winning Game

If anyone has made you believe that you are not up to the challenge of educating your own children without school, I am here to tell you that you are. You were your child's first teacher and you know your child better than anyone other than that child. In partnership with your child, you can do this. You are both wired to learn and when you open your mind to the small inner voice of wisdom, you will know what to do in any moment. And you will operate from a place of love. What a gift to your child!

I learned from one of my coaches that we are all playing a game of life. It is up to us to choose how we design that game. Now, I know that your child's education is important. And if we set up this game correctly, you will see that there is no way that you or your child can lose. Unfortunately, many parents simply try to reproduce school at home and that is a tough game to win. So, let's get started.

Your Relationship to Your Child Is Most Important

I learned from Brent Cameron that families are the smallest learning unit, not the individual. Children learn constantly from what their parents and siblings do. We learn in relationships with other people. We have a strong need to belong to a community. We are wired for relationships!

It is important for your child to know that they matter, they have natural gifts and talents, they don't have to be good at everything, they create their own world and their work is to share their gifts with the world.

If we feel safe and loved, our brain specializes in cooperation, play, and exploration! If we are constantly feeling unloved, frightened or unwanted, the brain specializes in managing feelings of fear and abandonment.
— Bessel Van Der Volk

Always act from love. That is the number one Universal Law. And this is especially true when parenting and guiding your children. Do not use coercion, threats, or rewards to get your son or daughter to do what you think they should do. You are the protector of their soul. Their soul is wise.

Shift from a Schooled to an Adventure Mindset

Schooling is a toxic mix of collectivism and egoism where separate students compete with each other by doing the same set of mundane tasks.

The collectivist mindset is taught in the unnatural learning environment of schooling. The economy is viewed as a fixed pie that needs to be distributed equally among all people (except for the elites who claim 99% of everything). What collectivists fail to understand is that men and women are creative beings. When a man or woman creates something, life appears differently. When an entrepreneur invents something or builds a company, the economy expands and there is more opportunity for everyone.

The egotistical mindset lends itself to distortion by narcissism as the world and economy is viewed as a zero-sum game. The individual wins only when others lose. Life is not cooperative, it is competitive.

Schooled Mindset	Adventure Mindset
Student as Object	Learner as Soul
Fear-based	Love-based
Outside-In Living	Inside-Out Living
Heavy Ecological Footprint	Light Ecological Footprint
Burnt Out	Resilient
Anxious	Peaceful
Depressed	Joyful
Compare and Compete	Look Inside
Special-Better	Unique-Equal
Consumer	Creator
Follower	Leader
Competitive	Cooperative
Striving	Flowing
Unconscious	Conscious
Reactive	Intentional
Low empathy for others	We're all in this together
Future focused	Present

Schooled Mindset: Belief that you are a separate mechanical being with a body that carries around a mechanical brain. Belief that the world is a cold, uncaring, mechanistic machine and that we are all separate. To survive, you need to strive and compete for scarce resources. You are in control. There is no higher power operating in the world.

Adventure Mindset: An adventure mindset acknowledges that we are spiritual beings having a human experience. We are constantly learning and growing. We are all animated by the same source of life. We are all connected to a universal mind that is the source of our insights, creativity, and imagination. Our essence is well-being, peace of mind, and joy that gets covered up by negative, fear-based thinking that has been conditioned into us.

An adventure mindset allows for the individual and the group Planet Earth to flourish. An adventure mindset incorporates what we know from quantum physics and consciousness research. The schooled mindset has been conditioned into you. Let it go right now.

Design Principles

Borrowing a page from design thinking, as you set out on your journey to design an educational environment and path for your children, it's helpful to have some design principles. These are some that I recommend you consider:

Love — Always make decisions and take actions from a place of love. If you are feeling frustrated, angry, overwhelmed, or anxious, then take a moment and let your thinking settle down before you talk to your child or make a decision. Take a walk, stretch, listen to music, just pause and let your mind settle and your natural state of peace return.

Trust— I think every home educating parent I have met has had moments of self-doubt. As your child transitions from one developmental stage to the next, oftentimes old interests are cast aside and new ones don't immediately appear. There might be moments of boredom and frustration. This is a great time to reach out to experienced home educators for reassurance and guidance. Trust the learning process. Trust your children.

Start When Your Child Asks — There is no research that shows any benefit to starting academic instruction at an early age. There is a lot of research that shows early education actually harms young men and women. Dr. Raymond Moore suggests that you start at 8 or 10. I don't think there is a formula that applies to all children. Mine followed their natural interests and were learning all the time - one with books and another with videos. Around 12 years old both wanted more structured academics and asked for it.

Guide — Don't Teach. Your child has everything inside to grow into an amazing adult. Like the acorn will grow into an oak tree, your child has the wisdom, resources, intelligence, and gifts to follow the soul's calling. Your work is to provide the best environment and curate resources to optimize the growth. You are like the gardener who is making sure the soil is rich, there is enough sun and rain. But you don't need to modify the seed. It is perfect.

Play — Humans learn so much from play. Play may look a lot different than when you were a child. Who is to say that playing the latest video game with friends is any less stimulating than playing chess?

Curiosity — Curiosity drives children to explore the world and figure out their place in it. My daughter coined a term when she was 4 years old: curiation which combines curiosity and imagination. Let your children play uninterrupted when they are younger and ask your children what they are curious about and what they are interested in learning and investing their time doing. Their answers might surprise you.

Imagination — Imagination is your connection to your divine powers of creation. Never, ever limit you son or daughter's imagination. Encourage it. Let it grow and expand. Encourage you son or daughter to imagine new worlds and infinite possibilities.

Non-Judgement — You are the space of impersonal awareness. This space does not judge. When your personal thinking starts judging your family's educational path or your child's choices as good or bad you will start feeling less free and stressed. It's okay. It is part of the journey.

Foster self-Agency — It is easy for adults to jump in and figure something out for younger people or try and solve situations. The more you can let your children find their own solutions and overcome their challenges, knowing that you've got their back, they will gain confidence in their own abilities and develop self-agency.

Creativity — We are born to create. Life is creative. We are part of life. Just look around you at the multitude of birds, plants, and animals. I believe that people are most happy and satisfied when they are creating in the way that they most enjoy. If you can view creating as your curriculum, you will never have a boring day.

The Natural Phases of De-Schooling

I co-created a coaching program for selfDesign in which we coached families around the world to home educate their children following a self-directed learning approach. After working with many families, I learned that there are natural phases of deschooling.

Phase One: Reproducing School at Home

Most parents who have moved from conventional schooling to homeschooling, try to reproduce all of the academics from school. Often, they will buy expensive, pre-packaged all-in-one curriculum or they will sign up for an expensive online school. From my direct experience and that of coaching other parents, the majority of homeschool curriculum is focused on information processing and memorization just like schooling and so is just as boring. I'll put my favorite home education resources in the Resource chapter so that you can pick and choose based on your child's interests and learning style.

Phase Two: Entering the Battle Zone

It is impossible to reproduce school at home because you don't have the methods of fear and shame that outside authorities wield. The sooner you give up this losing battle the better.

Giving Up

Many parents will swing to the other extreme after heated battles and bruised relationships. They just let their kids do whatever they want without any boundaries or restrictions. Often this looks like playing video games all day or being on electronics. Then the parents have moments of extreme self-doubt and insecurity and will swing back to school at home. This pendulum may swing many times until they relax into an eclectic, self-directed approach.

Beginning Anew: The Quilt Method

I love the book, Composing a Life, by Mary Catherine Bateson. She uses the analogy of a quilt as your life. You are always working on one square but, often until you get to the end, and see the beautiful quilt you have created, you're not sure where all of the pieces fit. And so it is with home educating. If you look at it as a messy, non-linear process of many fits and starts, a process of creative invention, then you will not be bothered with the box of unfinished projects sitting in your garage. You will not be plagued by the tyranny of the paper trail that you might think you need to prove that learning is happening. Allow your child to be guided by their soul, set boundaries on technology and social media, then enjoy the natural learning process.

Practice the Art of Self Direction

The focus of my work in education both at home and creating alternative learning experiences has been around self-direction. I created an entire online course on Self Directed Learning for the California Teachers College which you can enroll in at CapriceLea.com. I will do my best to make this section short and sweet.

One of the biggest misunderstandings about self-directed learning is that it means a child is learning alone. Nope. A child is choosing how to invest her time and often it will involve group classes, working with mentors, and sometimes doing conventional academics that looks very much like school.

How does one become self directed? People are naturally self directed especially when they are engaged in activities that they enjoy. Sage has been super self directed over the years as she has taught herself to do complicated hairstyles, makeup, and crafting by watching YouTube videos. I could never teach her these, because I have no personal interest and also no innate talent for it.

She is less self directed when it comes to something that she believes she should do but doesn't really want to do, for example math. So, the question then becomes, "why do you want to learn math and how can we make that happen?" Her answer was that she wanted to do the math classes necessary to get into a good college. So, she did algebra 1, geometry, and algebra 2 and next year will be doing an online college calculus class to get it out of the way. I talk frequently about how useless algebra 2 is for most people and since it was important to Sage to check off the box, it was a meaningful experience for her. And I'm happy to say that our relationship survived me tutoring her through the class.

Sage told me when she was 9 years old that she wanted someone to design her learning projects for her and then give her the freedom to complete the projects the way that she wanted to. She liked hands-on learning, games, and puzzles, and I found lots of fun things for her to do. It was a process of trial and error, strewing interesting things around the house, and being willing to abandon a project when it wasn't going well.

When she turned 13, she wanted more academics. We chose Acellus Academy because it is video based and offers instant feedback in the form of quizzes and tests. It looks very much like school online and it worked for Sage. She also took courses at the local community college to get early college credits. A significant portion of her time is invested at her dance studio and now at her part-time job.

My youngest daughter invests her time reading, writing, singing, acting, playing with friends, and cooking. She really doesn't like math, so we do it together to make sure she has basic numeracy to get along in life. She enjoys learning through books and workbooks, and hates doing video lessons. When she was 7 years old, I got her the Basher Science series of books and she learned about the human body, planet earth, and chemistry in a way that was interesting and engaging for her. At 12 years old, I would take her to the local bookstore, and she would choose Shakespeare and mystery novels. She loves to write and won a Daughters of the American Revolution essay contest. But when she was in public school for 7th grade, she started hating writing, reading, and music - all of her former and now recovered passions.

Different Ages and Stages of Learning

There is no timetable for learning. You don't want to glue wings to a caterpillar, as Brent Cameron pointed out in his critique of schooling. Do not view babies and young children as immature, defective adults. Recent studies have found that, in some ways, young children are smarter than adults.

Infants and young children are not just sitting twiddling their thumbs, waiting for their parents to teach them to read and do math. They are expending a vast amount of time and effort in exploring and understanding their immediate world. Healthy education supports and encourages this spontaneous learning.

— *David Elkind*

Babies

Babies know more than we think they do. This doesn't mean that they need artificial activities or make work. Children under the age of five are not good at making plans or focusing on goals. They are busy getting to know their environment and are in awe and wonder about everything. Let them stay enchanted with the natural world. The young brain has many more neurons than adult brains[86]. It is plastic and flexible. Just allow babies to play and create a safe environment for open exploration.

You work at this stage is to make sure your son or daughter feels unconditional love and completely safe. Do not use technology as a babysitter. Technology is negatively impacting minds and limiting sensory input by making us focus on a narrow window of experience.

Ages 2-7: Let them Play, Explore & Be in Nature

Young children learn through play. They learn to cooperate, negotiate, and solve conflicts. Children learn how the world works. They watch adults and then pretend to do what they do. Pre-schoolers have been observed using probability and imagination to predict outcomes.

If you are not familiar with the work of Raymond S. Moore, I highly encourage you to read his book, Better Late Than Early[87]. He makes a compelling case for not doing ANY academic work before the ages of 8-10. He shows evidence that most of the "disabilities" in reading and math are due to forcing children to do this work before they are ready. Some of his recommendations seem a bit too prescriptive to me, given that every man and woman is a unique expression of the divine. He does provide a fresh take on the developmental stages and what you can expect as your son or daughter gets older. I agree that early schooling is harmful and encourage you to do academics when your child starts asking for them. Raymond Moore says not before the age of 8 or 10. Schools in Finland start at age 8. Scientific evidence support started education later. There is no evidence that early childhood schooling is beneficial.

The conviction that the best way to prepare children for a harsh, rapidly changing world is to introduce formal instruction at an early age is wrong. There is simply no evidence to support it, and considerable evidence against it. Starting children early academically has not worked in the past and is not working now.

— David Elkind

Psychologist Peter Gray, author of Free to Learn88, is an expert in learning through play. I highly recommend you check out his excellent articles on his Psychology Today blog. As Peter Gray demonstrates, young children learn the skills to function in their environment through voluntary, self-directed, unstructured play when there is no pressure to perform or be creative.

Children under the age of 5 tend to learn a foreign language more quickly than older children and adults. So, if you know a foreign language, speak it to them.

Again, do not use technology as a babysitter.

Ages 8-12: Projects Rule

The Wondertree Center was divided into broad age brackets: Age 5, 6-8, 9-12, and 13+. These groupings were based on Brent's experience with the changing interests and abilities of learners. In Finland, schools begin formal math instruction with children at the age of 8. Brent also found that around that age, many children are eager for more conceptual learning. This is no hard and fast rule. As we saw in the Science of Individuality and There is No Average, each child comes with their own propensity and wiring for learning.

I did see an intellectual blossoming and emotional maturation around the age of 8 and 9. These are the early bridge years between being young children who love free play and exploration and children who want to learn more about the world and their place in it. We did lots of science experiments, geocaching, and I started a self-directed learning center for ages 8-13. We brought in an art teacher and partnered with a nature teacher to take the kids on excursions one afternoon a week. Projects varied by the week and were inspired by the interests of the kids and the mentors. The kids love doing walkabouts in the community and exploring their place in it.

When given a choice of how to invest their time, these learners wanted to be active, outside, and part of the community. I highly recommend at this age to find places where they can contribute their gifts and feel like valuable members of the community, whether it is volunteering on a local farm, animal shelter, or other business.

Ages 13+: Give them Freedom and Have Lots of Conversations

Around the age of 12 or 13, many kids want to do more focused work. This is when, if they have had enough time to play, discover, and just be, they tend to want to do more deep learning and some more academic pursuits.

My oldest daughter decided she wanted to make sure she was at grade level in all of her high school work. Checking off the boxes was important to her. That might not look like self-direction to some people, and all of her academic choices were self-chosen. She liked some classes (history) better than others (math, chemistry). It was important that she stayed true to herself and followed her inner knowing. She will be graduating high school with 10 college credits.

I have discovered how important it is for me to be there as a loving, non-judgmental guide to help them transition into adulthood. No conversation is off limits. I've heard about all of the shenanigans of other teenagers. I'm not a perfect mother; there is no perfect parent. By allowing my daughters to self-direct their learning, they have learned to self-direct their lives. They don't engage in any self-destructive behavior because they have nothing to rebel against. And we moved through and healed from an extremely traumatic divorce when I found out their father was seeing other women. He made choices that didn't include our daughters' well-being. It was a rough patch and love and openness got us through to a place where we are all thriving.

I learned that it's not my job to protect my kids from life. Life is a full-contact sport. My work is to help them gracefully navigate it, connected to the inner wisdom and using their imagination to create what they want.

What is Worth Learning?

The best way to approach learning design and curriculum is to realize that most textbooks and curricula are inherently boring, fact-based, and often inaccurate. Free yourself from the tyranny of textbooks. The textbook industry is big business and one of the main reasons that there is no innovation in school. That said, there are lots of new and engaging learning resources that you can use with your children. I have put links to resources I like on my website CapriceLea.com.

The 7 Liberating Arts & Sciences

I highly recommend that you do some research on the classical approach to learning before you assume that the Western model of schooling is sufficient. The 7 Liberating Arts and Sciences include the Trivium (letters, quality, and mind) and the Quadrivium (numbers, quantity, and matter).

There are amazing free resources at TriviumEducation.com that include free study materials and great podcasts with Gene Odening. You don't teach your kids the Trivium as much as learn it yourself so that it shifts your view of the world and learning.

For example, Gene Odening shares in a podcast how his mother taught him the parts of speech while driving to school in the morning. She would point out things and have him label them to introduce nouns. The next day, she would point out actions to introduce verbs. Such a practical and easy approach to learning! So much more interesting than endless, repetitive worksheets.

The Trivium starts with Grammar, which is the who, what, where, and when of a subject. This is a far more logical and useful approach to grammar than I learned with sentence diagramming and memorizing the parts of speech conceptually. After Grammar comes Logic, the why of a subject. By studying logic, you realize how illogical most of what we are told truly is. Rhetoric comes next and it is the ability to put together a sound oral or written argument. The goal of the Trivium is the generation of wisdom.

The Quadrivium consists of Arithmetic, Geometry, Music and Astronomy. I am in the process of educating myself with the 7 Liberating Arts and Sciences. Going through this process has made me realize what a complete waste of time and energy my schooling was. I am highly schooled and poorly educated. And I am taking full responsibility for my own education. A great place to start is Dorothy Sayers essay *The Lost Tools of Learning*.

Most of What We've Been Taught is False

I am going to repeat what I put in the foreword here. Over the course of the past three years, I have come to realize that almost everything that I was taught in school was false. Perhaps there were a few truths sprinkled in so that the narratives I was being taught weren't completely absurd, but I now realize that mostly everything I was taught about history, science, how the universe works, how the human body works, religion, and who and what I am are false. These false narratives add up to a disempowering, nihilistic worldview that denies the primacy of human imagination and creativity.

Most of the curriculum, even homeschooling curriculum, that you will find is based on the dead ideas of Humanism and Scientism. Even if you find history that looks "patriotic" it is probably based on a false Hegelian dialectic intended to divide and conquer the people.

I invite you to check out the resource page on CapriceLea.com to find resources that inspire curiosity and discovery of the truth.

There Are No Basics

My own experience, as well as that of other researchers, suggests that rather than creating enthusiasm and stimulating thinking, textbooks usually deaden the minds of students and alienate them from learning.

— Mordechai Gordon

There is so much information currently in the world, you can't even hope to learn 1%. There are no basics. The Common Core was invented by people with no education background. They were bureaucrats and politicians, not teachers. If you let go of the mistaken notion that there is a fixed set of information your kid needs to become an adult, then life gets a whole lot simpler and more fun.

I remember when Kayli was 5 years old, she became fascinated with animals. If anyone in the family had any questions about animals, she was our go-to person. She was equipped with lots of books on animals and an iPad. She became fascinated with sharks, so we binge watched shark week. She became entranced with science, so we got the Basher science series and she told me all about the b-cells and t-cells that heal our bodies. This is how learning happens. In the free inquiry of a relaxed, playful mind.

Contrast that with Kayli's experience of public school 7 years later. She started hating her favorite pastimes - reading, writing, and music. She sat there day after day as they tried to stuff her full of information that she was neither interested in nor cared about. As the end of school approached and the state standardized test loomed ever closer, the pace of this information stuffing became frenetic. The teachers got increasingly stressed. It was a mess. All for a test that somebody made up. It is absurd to think that all 12-year olds need to know certain things that most adults probably don't know which will be forgotten by next year.

The Smorgasbord Approach

Okay, I'm 25% Danish and love smorgasbords where you can choose a little bit of lots of different foods to eat. This is a great way to introduce the world to your child.

Your child will tell you when they are ready for or interested in something. View yourself as the guide along the side and the curator of cool resources. If your child is interested in something, then make sure he has the resources, mentors, and support to pursue that interest. A wonderful way to introduce new things is to strew books and fun resources around the house for your child to discover. Another way is to be actively engaged in creative projects that you love to model creating as learning.

When Sage wanted to learn to play the guitar, I found an inexpensive electric guitar and we tried several guitar teachers until she found one that she clicked with. Sometimes you need to try many mentors until you find the right one for your kid. Also, many adults act differently when they are with adults than when they are one-on-one with children. Teach your kids to trust their intuition about people.

Reading

Once again, don't think that you need to reproduce schooling when it comes to teaching reading. The majority of kids learn to read when they are interested and ready. A friend of mine who specialized in teaching Gifted students told me that gifted kids either learn to read early (before the age of 5) or late (after the age of 12). The range of ages when a child learns to read is quite wide. It is simply not true that every child should be reading at age 5.

I worked with a Special Education teacher at selfDesign who was also a reading specialist. She told me that 30% of kids need help learning to read. Here is a quick test to see if your child is struggling with reading and needs help. If you child wants to read and asks for help, then get help. If they are not interested in reading, then make sure you have an environment at home that treasures reading. Read a lot by yourself and to your child. If you do decide to teach reading, don't use whole word instruction. I'll explain more later.

My youngest loves to read and always had her nose in a book since she was 7 years old. She read the Harry Potter series 3 times before she was 9. And she started to hate reading in public school. Have you ever had to read something and annotate it? That is almost a sure-fire way to kill the love of reading. Here's my recommendation: read around your kids if you love to read. Have a house that supports literacy. Read to them a lot when they are young. Allow them to read what they want to read.

Dyslexia

My oldest daughter is dyslexic. She has no phonemic awareness, which means that she cannot sound out words. Home educating your child is one of the best things you can do if your child is dyslexic. The current Diagnostic and Statistical Manual of Mental Disorders (DSM–5) took out dyslexia as a diagnosis, so if you do take your child to be assessed, the psychologist will give a diagnosis of a specific learning disability in reading and writing.

I think that viewing dyslexia as a disability is disempowering. Sir Richard Branson, himself dyslexic agrees. He says, "Dyslexic minds have exactly the skills we need for the workforce of tomorrow". He attributes his success in business to his dyslexia. He was a poor student in school and wildly successful in life. He has funded the creation of MadeByDyslexia.com which has some wonderful videos.

When my daughter was 5 years old, she asked me for reading glasses because she said her eyes weren't working. She really wanted to read. A normal eye exam showed she was slightly far-sighted which was normal for her age. I then took her to two developmental ophthalmologists who recommended extensive and expensive eye exercises in their office. We tried them. She hated them. They gave her intense headaches. There is conflicting research on whether or not developmental eye exercises help or not.

We did not figure out that she was dyslexic until she was 13 despite her getting an IEP when she was 7 from our local school district's psychologist. The remediation they recommended at that time did not work.

If your child asks for support, like mine did, get your child tested to see if they have phonemic awareness. We consulted lots of reading and dyslexia specialists. I'm not sure why nobody tested her until she was 13 for phonemic awareness, the classic definition of dyslexia.

Many people recommend Orton-Gillingham. It didn't work for us because it is task-oriented, sequential, and boring. Sage is a right-brain visual learner who learns by seeing the big picture first and then fitting the pieces in. Pretty much the opposite of all Orton-Gillingham approaches. Sage did work with a woman who was getting her PhD in Special Education with a focus on reading for 1.5 years. They painstakingly went through all of the phonemes so that Sage could memorize and pronounce them. It helped a little bit. It wasn't the magic bullet.

What we've done is helped Sage focus on her strengths. Manipulation of language and symbols isn't her strength. Sage reads slowly but competently and prefers video courses over textbooks or lectures.

If your child struggles with reading, do some research on famous and successful people with dyslexia who succeed because they have other strengths. Many wildly successful people including Paul Orfalea, Sir Richard Branson, Thomas Edison, Henry Ford, Ted Turner and even Albert Einstein have/had dyslexia. Every child is unique, and there is no one approach that works for everyone. Just remember, as you try different approaches: your child is not broken.

Writing

Some kids love to write, others hate it, many are neutral. My youngest daughter loves to write but this love of writing was almost wiped out in her year of public school because of their focus on the mechanics of writing and vocabulary rather than the creativity of writing and the importance of communication.

Sage took ENG 101 and 102 at our local community college as a high school junior last year. She got a 100 in both classes. Her instructor was more focused on a student's ability to communicate and think. She does both well. She writes like she speaks in a very conversational and easy to read way.

As with reading, the focus is on communicating ideas. Today, the ability to do videos and podcasts is just as valid a skill as writing. There are fabulous writing programs including Brave Writer and Cover Story that make writing fun and relevant.

Mathematics

I have met so many successful entrepreneurs who confess to me in hushed tones that they couldn't do school math. Yet, here they are, running a business, managing cash flow, and balancing their book. We are not taught real or practical math in school. Many adults cannot do elementary level school math. An informal Buzzfeed quiz[89] found that their staff got a 50% on basic math questions. These are successful, employed adults so it begs the question of the usefulness of most school math.

Math is the subject that homeschooling families struggle with the most. This is mainly because school math is not real math. And the math you will find on standardized tests is also different from school math. School math is designed to make you feel dumb.

If your child is heading to college, it helps to know that Algebra is the most frequently failed course in high school and community college. There is a movement afoot to get rid of Algebra as a requirement. While algebra is foundational for advanced, conceptual math, statistics and data science are often more useful for many professions.

To start this conversation, I invite you to read A Mathematician's Lament by Paul Lockhart. It is a wonderful essay on how school math destroys the love of mathematics and doesn't help children appreciate the beauty of math. I've linked to it in the End Notes and on my resources page at CapriceLea.com.

When you start studying sacred geometry, quantum arithmetic, and numerology, you notice that the universe does indeed operate according to God's laws. There is nothing random in nature. Life is beautiful, complex, and orderly.

Neither of my children were doing grade-level math throughout elementary school or middle school because it wasn't enjoyable for them and it wasn't an interest. And when it came time to do Algebra 1, Geometry, and Algebra 2, my daughter did just fine and got A's in all of her online courses. What school doesn't tell you is that an Algebra 1 class will go over all of the skills a child needs for that course. And by the time you get to these higher-level courses, they are allowed to use a calculator. As long as your child understands the concept of multiplication and division, they will not need to do procedures like long division. Think about it... how often do you do long division? I usually just open my smartphone and use the calculator.

Here are my favorite ways to explore the beauty of mathematics:

- Playing store with play money
- Board and Card Games
- Constructing the Universe by Michael S. Schneider
- Sacred Geometry
- Quantum Arithmetic

We did math games and songs when they were younger. We cooked together and played with fractions. My daughter is doing an online college Calculus class her Senior year of high school to get it out of the way and because you only pay for it if you pass. I figure they've put a lot of time and effort into producing a quality class that young people will pass. I will put my favorite resources in the appendix for you.

For your design process, think about the math that you use on a daily basis. Fractions are helpful for cooking. Counting money is necessary for shopping. Measuring is needed for sewing and building. Trigonometry is useful if you are making furniture. Data science is necessary so that you can analyze news reports and see if data is being manipulated to support someone's opinion. Dividing fractions? Geometric proofs?

One of my favorite math resources is Constructing the Universe by Michael S. Schneider. He wrote a book by the same name and activity books that take you through each number one through nine to appreciate math in the context of nature, art, and architecture.

One of my favorite math resources is Stanford Professor, Jo Boaler's, YouCubed website. Dr. Boaler specializes in teaching math teachers how to teach math. I took the beta version of her parent course when it first came out and it was transformational in helping me to reframe math. Here are some things that I learned:

• Embrace mistakes: Making a mistake on a math problem is the best way to grow your brain.
• Timed math tests are one of the worst things on the planet.
• Math is best learned cooperatively so that children can see there are many different ways to solve the same problem.

On her YouCubed website, there is a course for students and lots of fun math tasks.

Science

It is important to understand the difference between Science and Scientism. Science is the direct exploration of nature to determine the Laws of Nature. Scientism is a religion that sells us false theories and mocks anyone who doesn't agree with them. Since when did Science claim that truth is final?

If I were going to educate my daughters all over again, I would have to completely redo our science education. Since I wrote *Instead of Schooling*, my beliefs in the big bang and evolution theory have been shattered. I've learned that the dinosaurs are a hoax.

What would I share with my daughters now? That the universe is electric, there are battling theories around health (germ theory vs. terrain theory), water is intelligent, plants and trees communicate with each other, bees don't fly (they vibrate at the rate of the earth and levitate), and so much more.

Since I am learning new ideas every day, I will put my science resources on my website so that I can update frequently.

I highly recommend that you just let your kids explore and stay in awe and wonder about the world around them. Plant a garden with your kids. Growing your own food is a great way to stay connected to nature. My youngest daughter was entranced by the Basher science books and spent most of her time in nature. Lots of hands-on experiments makes science real.

I am currently engaged in developing an education ministry for learners of all ages, with one focus being to guide people to go out into nature and explore the Laws of Nature through direct experience. We don't want to replace one set of beliefs with another. We want people to fall in love with the earth again and marvel at her miracles.

My daughters loved science and exploring the natural world until they got a taste of school science. School science is trapped by the materialist, reductionist paradigm. It teaches the parts of a plant but not the magnificence of plants. It fails to teach that plants are the most efficient creations and can communicate between each other.

Economics

I understand the financial system, banking, and money now that the corruption of our institutions is in plain sight. You cannot function well as an adult without an understanding of money, finances, and economics. Trust me on this one. I have an MBA in finance from Carnegie Mellon University and received a scholarship my second year there for best female student in finance. My economics classes at Carnegie Mellon were calculus based. I even dreamed Calculus my first few months there. Pretty scary! But they didn't teach me the truth. I was grateful to have taken a course at Carnegie Mellon taught by Herbert Simon who won a Nobel Prize for Economics. I will never forget Dr. Simon telling my class, "the only function of government is to reallocate income". That has always stuck with me.

I now understand that our economy runs of debt slavery. I've realized that the big battle between Keynes and Von Mises was just theater. They are both eugenicists. It's also important to understand how our monetary system works (or doesn't work).

Most people don't understand that our whole monetary system is based on debt. Money is created when an individual, company, organization, or government institution takes out a loan. When you investigate the history of money, your view of the whole system changes. I include some of these resources on my website.

This was one of my only non-negotiables for my daughters. I wasn't going to let them enter adulthood without a solid foundation in economics. My personal understanding of economics is that innovation and entrepreneurship happen at the individual level.

Governments and bureaucracies are not innovative. They do not create jobs. They create nothing. There is a role for government, but it is not creating or growing businesses. Federal and state governments collect taxes and then divvy up the money. Bureaucrats take the pie and cut it into slices. Entrepreneurs build businesses. When a person creates a business, jobs are created. The whole pie grows bigger. Few entrepreneurs are greedy capitalists. Most start their business because they have a great idea and a burning passion to make it real. There are easier ways to make money than starting a business.

I will include some great resources for you to explore for yourself.

History and Government

I am grouping these two subjects together because I now understand that history is re-written by the victors. All of the history and government education that we get is intended to prop up our current government and justify their past actions. There are a lot of brilliant men and women who are reconstructing history as best they can using source documents.

I started figuring this out when I was deconstructing the fable of Christopher Columbus.

As you delve into the resources that I provide on my website, remember that almost everything we have been taught is false. Go into this area of study with an "I don't know" attitude.

One of my favorite resources is the work of Matthew Ehret and Cynthia Chung at the Rising Tide Foundation. Matthew Ehret has written an awesome series of books called "The Clash of the Two Americas" that you can get on CanadianPatriot.org.

Learning Goals – A Flexible Living Plan

SelfDesign uses mind maps to help learners access their creative right brain to design a learning plan for the year. The intention is to tap into a learner's inner knowing and transcend their "shoulds" and intellect. Tony Buzan was the inventor of Mind Maps and his organization offers a free introductory course on mind mapping.

I saw that this works well for some kids and other kids aren't so excited by the prospect. I found lying on the floor with my children and a big sheet of paper, colored markers, and intensely curious and playful minds helped to start the conversation.

In August and September, there is a natural rhythm of renewal and excitement. Ask your child questions that spark great conversations:

"How do you want to invest your time?"
"What questions do you have about the world?"
"What do you enjoy doing?"

Be in a space of loving, impersonal non-judgement - which is who you really are. When you don't judge playing chess as more important and valid than playing video games, then your child will feel free to be exactly who they are in this moment. When you can let go of the unnatural timetable that schooling has imposed on learning, you rest easy in knowing that your child cannot fall behind because learning is not a race.

The important part of this process is putting your child in the middle and designing learning experiences around the child. Start with a beginner's mind. Admit that you don't know what will appear.

Don't try to force your kid into a pre-packaged curriculum. It looks like it is the easy answer at first. But I have yet to meet a child for which this approach really works.

The Importance of Rhythm

It is incredibly important to establish a rhythm for the days and weeks. I love the book, A Child's Seasonal Treasury by Betty Jones. As a seasoned Waldorf educator, she provides lots of songs, rituals, poems, games, and crafts to celebrate the changing of the natural seasons. It works spectacularly with young children.

I created large, color-coded wall calendars to help my daughters navigate the days. We had breakfast and lunch together and they worked on individual projects when I worked, because I have been a working, home educating mom since my daughters were born. And I have been fortunate to be able to work from home.

You will fall into a rhythm as you notice what makes sense. And some days, the rhythm just doesn't seem to work. Everything seems like it happens on the off-beat. We all have those days. I generally avoided the blogs of the moms who seemed like they had everything together and their homes and homeschool rooms looked picture perfect. It's awesome if that's how you roll. I didn't.

Reverse Engineer Education

Don't make going to college the end goal.

As I showed previously, the   return on investment (ROI) of college is not always positive. One of the best alternatives is starting your own company or freelance business. It's interesting that college seems to be preparing people for jobs that no longer exist or are quickly disappearing, like college professors.

If college does make sense on your son or daughter's life journey, then one of the greatest benefits of learning outside of conventional schooling is that kids can start getting college credits so that they can lower their cost of college and graduate much earlier.

Most states offer free or reduced tuition to high school students who are doing dual enrollment at a community college. I recommend that if your child is doing dual enrollment, start with the common general education courses that are the cash cow, big lecture classes for most colleges. You can see a list of General Education or Core Curriculum requirements at every college website. They vary widely across colleges and some GE requirements cannot be satisfied by dual enrollment courses.

My oldest daughter did a mix of college classes at the local community college and online college classes during her junior and senior years of high school. She completed two semesters of college credit and entered as a sophomore.

Transfer of college credits is an interesting game. As long as you understand that the big freshman lecture courses are cash cows for colleges, you understand why they may not be overly excited about letting your kid opt out of them. That said, there are many colleges that are flexible and accommodating.

Jennifer Cook-DeRosa runs Homeschooling for College Credit and has Facebook groups that are specific to each state. This is a wonderful resource to get all of your questions answered.

Many students study for the College-Level Examination Programs (CLEP) or DSST, which are college-level tests that can be taken for college credit. Before you choose this path, it is helpful to know if your colleges of choice accept CLEP and/or DSST credits.

Avoid the Ten Biggest Blocks to Learning

Below are some of the biggest things that block the free flow of learning.

Fear: If you are feeling fearful, your kids will automatically pick up on it and become fearful themselves, So, when your inner GPS tells you that you are believing fearful thinking, pause and let your mind settle down.

Shame: Shame is the mistaken belief that "I am not good/worthy/lovable/smart." Because kids have been taught to compare themselves with others in school and to compete for the GPA, they often feel shame when they are not good at something or don't think that they compare favorably to their peers. Reassure them that the only person they are competing with is the self. Focus on excellence, not competing with others. Are they doing better today than yesterday? Is this something that they really care about and want to get good at?

Grades: Grades are silly. They don't accurately measure learning or capability. The top private schools in the country are currently engaged in an effort to replace grades with a Mastery Transcript. The state where we home educate requires letter grades for K-8 and then numeric grades and class ranking for grades 9-12. My daughters and I hold the grades lightly and know that they are not a measure of self-worth or innate capacity.

Comparison: Comparison is always a losing game. It is an instant joy killer. It will always get you tangled in a mess of negative thinking. Don't compare yourself to anyone else and don't compare your kids to anyone.

Time Pressure: Jo Boaler who teaches teachers how to teach math at Stanford says that timed math tests are the absolute worst way to learn maths. Timed tests of any sort are silly. Timetables for learning anything are also unscientific and invalid. The only cognitive task that a child needs to learn by a certain age is to learn to speak. If this is delayed, other skills will be delayed or more difficult. Let your sons and daughters learn at their own pace guided by their inner wisdom. It really doesn't matter how old they are when they learn certain things. When something is relevant to their lives, they will dig in and learn it in a fraction of the time it would take if you forced them to learn it when they are neither interested nor ready.

Rote Memorization: It is helpful to have some things stored in our memory banks, like addresses, phone numbers, birthdays, recipes, etc. Memorization is a small sliver of the learning process. If you are using a curriculum that focuses mainly on filling your son or daughter with information that they need to regurgitate, I would invite you to find a learning resource that is actually about learning not memorizing.

Sitting Still: We are designed to move. Research has found that engaging the body during the learning process is not just helpful, it is required. Let your kids move when they want to move. It doesn't mean that they have ADHD, they are alive, energetic beings. Neurophysiologist and educator Carla Hannaford wrote a wonderful book on the subject called Smart Moves.

Focus on Mechanics Instead of Meaning: If you focus on "doing it right" instead of having fun doing it, you will kill the love of learning. Just like my daughter Kayli loves reading and writing, but learned to hate it in school, focusing on mechanics stifles the love of learning. Humans need to understand the relevance of something and make it meaningful to enjoy doing it. Parents continually asked Michael Jordan how to make their sons great basketball players. His response was always, "Let them learn to love basketball."

Mismatch of Learning Experience with Learning Style: This is a big one! When my daughters were younger, we each did the Self-Portrait™ Power Traits Assessment. It was so helpful to figure out that they learned differently than I did. Somehow, it made my journey lighter and more fun. I realized I wasn't in charge. My oldest daughter learns through performing and doing. My youngest learns through reading and doing. I learn through reading and doing as well but with distinct differences.

10 Principles for Soul Guided Learning & Living

If I were going to create a Living Education Network, I would include the following organizations and resources that all align with the following principles.

1. Life is creative, adaptive, and self-organizing.

2. We use our minds, creativity, and energy to co-create a world for the maximum benefit of all life.

3. We are united around a shared cause of protecting all men and women's innate genius, imagination, and creativity.

4. Relationships are at the center of life.

5. Learning is emergent and soul-directed, not prescribed or predetermined.

6. The focus of learning is mastery of self and holistic wellbeing.

7. Critical thinking and morality are developed through free inquiry into areas of interest.

8. The definition of success expands to include the impact an individual has on the whole, including other people and the biosphere. Personal excellence replaces unbridled individual competition.

9. Experiences and relationships are valued over the accumulation of stuff.

10. We invest our time, energy, and money in our local communities.

My Self-Directed Education Journey

I am not anti-education. I am highly schooled -- with an MBA in finance from Carnegie Mellon and a BA from the University of Virginia. I now see through the illusion of schooling. I see it for what it is. It is not education; it is social engineering.

My home education journey started when I when I was two months pregnant with my first child. I was an older mom at 35 and was super excited to be having a baby. And then I had this terrible, scary thought. "What am I going to do for my son or daughter's schooling?" I had succeeded at school even though I hated it and was bored silly. College and grad school were better experiences for me, but I felt like I was stumbling around trying to figure out who I was and what I wanted to do with my life.

As I started doing research about alternatives to school, I came upon a speech given by John Taylor Gatto in 1989 when he was named NYC's Teacher of the Year after 30 years of teaching. It blew my mind. Before reading this, I hadn't considered that there were any alternatives to school. Below is an excerpt as published in Sun Magazine[90].

All of my years of sitting in class watching the second hand move slowly around the clock suddenly made sense. I vowed that my kids would discover who they were and what their gifts and talents were so that they could avoid a mid-life crisis and not waste the first 20 or so years of their lives.

I have come to realize that my main motivation in keeping my kids out of school went beyond the fact that I hated school and was intensely bored by it: I didn't want my kids to be institutionalized. And I always understood that we are social beings who want to be part of a larger community. In the past twenty years, I started many group learning environments to make sure my daughters and other young men and women had a place to gather, play, and learn together.

In 2004, I co-founded a democratic Sudbury school in North Carolina with three other families. Sudbury schools advocate self-direction for young men and women. It is a place where freedom is earned through demonstrations of responsibility. I learned that it is difficult for most parents to trust their kids because they have been trained not to trust themselves. Parents got nervous at the freedom that kids were given and did not understand that freedom comes with a great deal of responsibility at a Sudbury school .

When I moved to California in 2007, I was determined to create a self-directed learning center that had the benefits of a Sudbury school without what I perceived as its deficits. That was when I read the book selfDesign: Nurturing Genius Through Natural Learning by Brent Cameron. His description of his Wondertree Center in Vancouver, British Columbia inspired me to pick up the phone and request a visit to this alternative learning center. What I loved about selfDesign is that it focused on the family as the learning unit and replaced the rules that were often quite burdensome in Sudbury (even though they were created by a student-run judiciary committee) with agreements. Several conversations later, I began working with Brent and the selfDesign Learning Foundation.

In 2011-12, I worked tirelessly to start two K-12 charter schools in California for selfDesign. The charter schools were based on selfDesign's award winning learner-centered educational philosophy and praxis with a focus on social entrepreneurship and community service.

I received $500,000 in highly competitive federal grants from the U.S. Department of Education to start the charter schools. I did my best to get them authorized. I had a perfect building and an amazing team of experienced educators and administrators by my side. We couldn't get it done. I had to turn away half a million dollars because the local school district and county office of education would not authorize these charter schools. When does an entrepreneur have funding but not permission?

"On the one hand, you have selfDesign which allows children to follow their interests and passion. On the other hand, you have the California Department of Education that requires all children to learn the same things at the same time. I don't think there is a match here... Inherently the idea that you are going to allow students to select their curriculum based on what they are passionate about, it's inherently contradictory to you have to learn these things and you have to learn them in this order." – Roger Rice, Assistant Superintendent, Ventura County Office of Education, February 25, 2012, Ventura County Board of Education public hearing on the appeal for selfDesign charter schools.

I found out that the charter school application process in the county where I was living was rigged. We didn't have a chance despite selfDesign's numerous awards, accolades and track record. The superintendent of Ojai Unified School District at the time, Hank Bangser, told me behind closed doors, "I see how selfDesign teaches kids to love learning, but I don't see how you cover all of the standards." I learned that child-centered, self-directed learning has no place in public schooling.

So, the charter school petitions were not authorized because school board members saw that selfDesign, which begins with children's interests and passions and then curates learning experiences and curriculum to meet standards was "inherently contradictory" with the California school system which requires all students to learn the exact same thing at the exact same time in a specified, sequential order. And, of course, for every student that attended one of the charter schools, the school district would lose $5,000.

This experience was disheartening and exhausting. I was unable to inject innovation into a school system that looks very much like a factory. So, my daughters continued to learn outside of public school, combining home education with attending self-directed learning centers.

My oldest daughter, now 21 years old, was home educated K-12 and got a free ride to the college of her choice. She attended for a semester, saw that most of her peers were there to party (even though it was a Christian school), and realized she was wasting her time and energy. She is now building her own company.

My youngest daughter, Kayli, chose to go to public school for 7th grade in 2017 to make friends. We had moved to a new place after I had gotten divorced and it was difficult to meet friends her age because they were all in school. My daughter chose to go to school and I supported her because she is the author of her own life.

She was a "successful" student. The administrators were shocked that she scored in the 97th percentile in English/Language Arts without having had any direct instruction or schooling up to that point. She made some good friends, got on the honor roll, got straight A's (except for a C in art), and joined the cheer team.

She found the schoolwork to be boring and the grind of make-work overwhelming. Our biggest challenge was to keep her from absorbing the fear and shame that were being used as weapons to control the kids and make them comply. My daughter began to fear:

- Being late -- her homeroom teacher would yell "Tardy!" at late students and shame them publicly,

- Going to school without her tablet fully charged -- she would get a tech demerit and too many would result in an office visit with the Principal.

- Having a uniform violation -- they would shame the female students and make them go home.

- Complaining about any assignment -- teachers would say, "life is hard, this is easy in comparison".

- A mean group of boys who bullied her -- the guidance counselor got numerous complaints from many 7th grade girls and said sexual harassment is "extremely common" in middle school. No remedy was offered and the boys were not reprimanded.

What she discovered is that the entire K-8 school was being run by fear and shame. The biggest source of her discomfort was that she could tell that none of the teachers cared about her. They didn't notice how she felt emotionally. The teachers just paid attention to her outputs. My daughter said, "As long as I was producing good numbers, they could care less how I was feeling." When she decided not to return for her 8th grade year, none of her teachers said anything to her.

She is now navigating the public high school and dual enrollment at a local college because it is her choice to do so. Since I have raised my daughters to be soul-directed, I respect the choices they make as long as they are not harming anyone. She chose to go to school because that is where most men and women her age spend their days. Because she was outside of the system for most of her life, she is able to see through it, navigate it, and make it work for her.

Addendum: Resources

There is an extensive list of carefully curated resources on the author's website at CapriceLea.com.

1:1 COACHING, ONLINE COURSES, & FREE LEARNING RESOURCES

Build the Life and Livelihood You Desire Without Stress or Suffering

Online Courses

Unlock Your Hidden Genius: to start a business outside of the matrix

Stress Relief 101: learn to flow with life

Self Directed Learning: step by step to unleash your children's genius & creativity

CapriceLea.com

Notes

[1] American Humanist Association. "Humanist Manifesto I." American Humanist Association, 12 July 2020, americanhumanist.org/what-is-humanism/manifesto1.

[2] American Humanist. "AHA_v._BOP_Final_Settlement_All_Signatures." American Humanist, Mar. 2017, Americanhumanist.org.

[3] https://www.pewresearch.org/religion/religious-landscape-study/, retrieved 02/24/23

[4] https://www.businessinsider.com/sherry-turkle-why-tech-moguls-send-their-kids-to-anti-tech-schools-2017-11

[5] https://www.youtube.com/watch?v=1TerTgDEgUE

[6] https://www.youtube.com/watch?v=JKHUaNAxsTg

[7] https://www.nature.com/articles/s41586-021-04269-6

[8] https://canadianpatriot.org/2023/01/23/the-keynes-vs-von-hayek-debate-a-false-dualism-with-malthusian-characteristics/

[9] https://canadianpatriot.org/2022/06/21/yuval-hararis-unipolar-dystopia-vs-the-greater-eurasian-partnership-two-technological-paradigms-clash/

[10] https://politicalvelcraft.org/2011/12/16/118-million-murdered-by-socialisms-main-three-soviet-socialism-chinese-socialism-and-german-socialism/

[11] Dewey, John, and Philip Jackson. The School and Society and The Child and the Curriculum (Centennial Publications of The University of Chicago Press). 1st ed., University of Chicago Press, 1991, p. 15

[12] https://www.nea.org/sites/default/files/2022-08/nea-resolutions_2022-2023.pdf

[13] https://www.technocracy.news/scientism-when-science-becomes-religion/

[14] https://youtu.be/NVoCtZga7qM

[15] Scientific American, November 2008, Does Nature Break the Second Law of Thermodynamics?, J. Miguel Rubí

[16] https://archive.org/details/final-warning-history-of-new-world-order-by-david-allen-rivera/page/114/mode/1up

[17] Itzkowitz, Michael. "Higher Ed's Broken Bridge to the Middle Class – Third Way." Third Way, 25 Sept. 2019, www.thirdway.org/report/higher-eds-broken-bridge-to-the-middle-class.

[18] https://www.consumerreports.org/student-loan-debt-crisis/

[19] https://www.wsj.com/articles/americans-are-losing-faith-in-college-education-wsj-norc-poll-finds-3a836ce1

[20] Gallup. "Student Enthusiasm Falls as High School Graduation Nears." Gallup, 1 June 2017, gallup.com.

[21] Organisation for Economic Co-operation and Development. "Programme for International Student Assessment (PISA) Results from PISA 2018." Https://Www.Oecd.Org/, 2019, www.oecd.org/pisa/publications/PISA2018_CN_USA.pdf

[22] "New Study of the Literacy of College Students Finds Some Are Graduating With Only Basic Skills." American Institutes for Research, 14 Sept. 2017, www.air.org/news/press-release/new-study-literacy-college-students-finds-some-are-graduating-only-basic-skills.

[23] Wylie Communications. "What's the Latest U.S. Literacy Rate?" Wylie Communications, Mar. 2019, www.wyliecomm.com/2019/03/us-literacy-rate.

[24] Gallup, "Student Enthusiasm Falls as High School Graduation Nears." Gallup, 1 June 2017, gallup.com.

[25] Wilson, Jackson, "Capturing students' attention: An empirical study", Journal of the Scholarship of Teaching and Learning, 12/01/2013

[26] Sparks, S. (2019, October 30), 'No Progress' Seen in Reading or Math on Nation's Report Card, Education Week, retrieved 11/17/19 from http://blogs.edweek.org/edweek/inside-school-research/2019/10/reading_math_NAEP_2019.html

[27] Consortium for Policy Research in Education. "Seven Trends: The Transformation of the Teaching Force." Cpre.Org, Apr. 2014, www.cpre.org/sites/default/files/workingpapers/1506_7trendsapril2014.pdf.

[28] https://www.jrbooksonline.com/PDF_Books/SecretsOfFedReserve.pdf

[29] https://www.cchr.org/documentaries/diagnostic-and-statistical-manual/, retrieved 02/24/23

30 https://www.cchr.org/documentaries/diagnostic-and-statistical-manual/watch.html, retrieved 3/22/23

31 Scientific American, October 2014, Why We Need to Abandon the Disease-Model of Mental Health Care.

32 Jeffreys, Sheila, The Transgendering of Children: Gender eugenics, Science Direct, retrieved 6/1/2023, https://www.sciencedirect.com/science/article/abs/pii/S0277539512000982

33 Post and Courier, MUSC ends hormone therapy for transgender kids following SC Statehouse conservative backlash, 12/19/2022, https://www.postandcourier.com/health/musc-ends-hormone-therapy-for-transgender-kids-following-sc-statehouse-conservative-backlash/article_9a3e2646-7fbf-11ed-a24c-8bbf3f1b0a57.html#newsletter-popup

34 Schlott, Rikki, "I literally lost organs", why detransitioned teens regret changing genders, NY Post, https://nypost.com/2022/06/18/detransitioned-teens-explain-why-they-regret-changing-genders/

35 https://www2.ed.gov/about/offices/list/ocr/docs/ed-factsheet-transgender-202106.pdf

36 https://www.innovationhub-act.org/cw-documents-0

37 https://www.innovationhub-act.org/sites/default/files/2021-03/Cognitive%20Warfare.pdf

38 https://digitalcommons.law.umaryland.edu/cgi/viewcontent.cgi?referer=&httpsredir=1&article=1136&context=mjil

39 https://www.stephanieboye.com/post/the-impact-of-porn-on-teens, retrieved 02/23/23

40 https://podclips.com/c/FCnqIJ, retrieved 02/23/23

41 Becker, Jeff. "NASA 'Brainwaves Reveal Student Engagement, Operate Household Objects.'" BrainCo, 21 June 2019, www.brainco.tech/blog/2015/03/02/gaining-exposure.

42 Robinson, Melia. "Tech Billionaires Spent $170 Million on a New Kind of School — Now Classrooms Are Shrinking and Some Parents Say Their Kids Are 'Guinea Pigs.'" Business Insider Nederland, 22 Nov. 2017, www.businessinsider.nl/altschool-why-parents-leaving-2017-11?international=true&r=US.

43 Strauss, Valerie. "Students Protest Zuckerberg-Backed Digital Learning Program and Ask Him: 'What Gives You This Right?'" Washington Post, 17 Nov. 2018, www.washingtonpost.com/gdpr-consent/?next_url=https%3a%2f%2fwww.washingtonpost.com%2feducation%2f2018%2f11%2f17%2fstudents-protest-zuckerberg-backed-digital-learning-program-ask-him-what-gives-you-this-right%2f, accessed 12/17/19

44 Carnegie Mellon University - Heinz College. "Building Effective Communications Around Student Data Privacy—Executive Summary." Https://Www.Studentprivacymatters.Org/, 2017, www.studentprivacymatters.org/wp-content/uploads/2017/12/CMU-survey-privacy-start-ups-2017.pdf.

45 https://www.davista.ai/school-safety.html

46 Beckett, Lois. "Clear Backpacks, Monitored Emails: Life for US Students under Constant Surveillance." The Guardian, 10 Dec. 2019, www.theguardian.com/education/2019/dec/02/school-surveillance-us-schools-safety-shootings.

47 Jackson, G. (2009). Drug-induced dementia: A perfect crime. As quoted in Colbert, T. The Four False Pillars of Biopsychiatry.

48 Bonawitz, E. et.al, The double-edged sword of pedagogy, https://pubmed.ncbi.nlm.nih.gov/21216395/

49 Maturana, Humberto. "Reflections by Humberto Maturana." Systemic Design, RSD5, Oct. 2016, systemic-design.net.

50 Cook Moats, Louisa. "The Missing Foundation in Teacher Education: Knowledge of the Structure of Spoken and Written Language." PA Coalition for World Class Math, The Greenwood Institute, paworldclassmath.webs.com/Missing%20Foundation%20(Moats).pdf. Accessed 12 July 2020.

51 Organisation for Economic Co-operation and Development. "Programme for International Student Assessment (PISA) Results from PISA 2018." Https://Www.Oecd.Org/, 2019, www.oecd.org/pisa/publications/PISA2018_CN_USA.pdf.

52 Wylie Communications. "What's the Latest U.S. Literacy Rate?" Wylie Communications, Mar. 2019, www.wyliecomm.com/2019/03/us-literacy-rate.

53 The Missing Foundation in Teacher Education: Knowledge of the Structure of Spoken and Written Language, Louisa Cook Moats, Annals of Dyslexia, 1994, https://paworldclassmath.webs.com/Missing%20Foundation%20(Moats).pdf, 12/29/19

54 https://www.maa.org/external_archive/devlin/LockhartsLament.pdf, retrieved 2/22/23

55 Callaway, Ewen Nature Magazine. "Fearful Memories Passed Down to Mouse Descendants." Scientific American, 1 Dec. 2013, www.scientificamerican.com/article/fearful-memories-passed-down.

56 Gordon, Mordechai. Ten Common Myths in American Education. Amsterdam-Netherlands, Netherlands, Amsterdam University Press, 2005, p. 37

57 https://digital.sciencehistory.org/works/cf95jc09d

58 Ibid, p. 41

59 https://www.businessinsider.com/infographic-the-odds-of-being-alive-2012-6

60 https://www.nature.com/articles/533452a

61 https://www.livescience.com/8365-dark-side-medical-research-widespread-bias-omissions.html

62 https://www.cchr.org/documentaries/diagnostic-and-statistical-manual/

63 https://libertarianinstitute.org/articles/sheldon/tgif-how-science-becomes-religion/

64 https://americanhumanist.org/what-is-humanism/manifesto2/

65 https://archive.org/details/new-world-order.-the-ancient-plan-of-secret-societies-by-still-william-t.-z-lib.org

66 Gallup, Inc. "How Many Americans Know U.S. History? Part I." Gallup.Com, 14 Nov. 2018, news.gallup.com/poll/9526/How-Many-Americans-Know-US-History-Part.aspx.

67 The National Education Association of the United States. "Cardinal Principles of Secondary Education: A Report, National Education Association of the United States. Commission on the Reorganization of Secondary Education." Internet Archive, 1918, archive.org/details/cardinalprinciploonatiuoft/page/14/mode/2up

68 American Council of Trustees and Alumni. "A Crisis in Civic Education." American Council of Trustees and Alumni, Jan. 2016, www.goacta.org.

69 https://www.newyorker.com/magazine/2008/11/10/suffering-souls, retrieved 02/24/23

[70] https://ttfuture.org/files/2/members/int_jcp_amazing.pdf, retrieved 3/23.

[71] https://themillenniumreport.com/2017/07/the-heart-is-not-a-pump, retrieved 3/23.

[72] When the Thyroid Speaks, the Heart Listens, Mark A. Sussman, 3 Apr 2018, Circulation Research. 2001;89:557–559, https://doi.org/10.1161/res.89.7.557

[73] Clerico A, Recchia FA, Passino C, Emdin M. Cardiac endocrine function is an essential component of the homeostatic regulation network: physiological and clinical implications. Am J Physiol Heart Circ Physiol. 2006 Jan;290(1):H17-29. doi: 10.1152/ajpheart.00684.2005. PMID: 16373590.

[74] https://www.scienceabc.com/pure-sciences/double-slit-experiment.html

[75] Cowan, Tom, Wise Traditions magazine, What Does — and Doesn't — Make Us Sick, Spring 2023.

[76] Zajonc, Arthur, Los Angeles Times, Seeing the Light, July 25, 1993, retrieved 05/30/23, https://www.latimes.com/archives/la-xpm-1993-07-25-tm-16606-story.html

[77] https://www.hilarispublisher.com/open-access/human-photosynthesis-a-turning-point-in-the-understanding-and-treatment-of-alzheimers-disease-1948-593X.1000079.pdf

[78] https://pubmed.ncbi.nlm.nih.gov/15947465/

[79] https://www.theguardian.com/environment/2020/apr/05/smarty-plants-are-our-vegetable-cousins-more-intelligent-than-we-realise

[80] https://e360.yale.edu/features/are_trees_sentient_peter_wohlleben

[81] Levy, Wetiko, p. 77

[82] Holt, J, The Mind is Not a Muscle, https://www.facebook.com/watch/?v=268044213903474

[83] http://carolblack.org/a-thousand-rivers, retrieved 3/19/2023

[84] "Roger J. Williams and the Science of Individuality." Mises Institute, 19 Aug. 2010, mises.org/library/roger-j-williams-and-science-individuality.

[85] https://www.ted.com/talks/sir_ken_robinson_do_schools_kill_creativity , retrieved 02/23/23

[86] Gopnik, Alison. "Your Baby Is Smarter Than You Think." Https://Www.Nytimes.Com/#publisher, 17 Aug. 2009, www.nytimes.com/2009/08/16/opinion/16gopnik.html?pagewanted=1&_r=2&th&emc=th.

87Moore, Raymond and Dorothy, Better Late than Early, 1975

88Gray, P. Free to Learn, 2013

89 Tanya Chen, "Here's What Happens When A Bunch Of Adults Try To Do Fifth-Grade Math." BuzzFeed, 18 Dec. 2013, www.buzzfeed.com/tanyachen/heres-what-happens-when-a-bunch-of-adults-try-to-do-5th-grad.

90 https://thesunmagazine.org/issues/175/why-schools-dont-educate